ABOUT THE ROYAL SHAKESPEARE COMPANY

The Shakespeare Memorial Theatre opened in Stratford-upon-Avon in 1879. Since then the plays of Shakespeare have been performed here, alongside the work of his contemporaries and of living modern playwrights. In 1960, the Royal Shakespeare Company was formed, gaining its Royal Charter in 1961. The founding principles of the Company were threefold: the Company would embrace the freedom and power of Shakespeare's work, train and develop young actors and directors and, crucially, experiment in new ways of making theatre. The RSC quickly became known for exhilarating performances of Shakespeare alongside new masterpieces such as *The Homecoming* and *Old Times* by Harold Pinter. It was a combination that thrilled audiences and this close and exacting relationship between writers from different eras has become the fuel that powers the creativity of the RSC.

In 1974, The Other Place opened in a tin hut on Waterside under the visionary leadership and artistic directorship of Buzz Goodbody. Determined to explore Shakespeare's plays in intimate proximity to her audience and to make small-scale, radical new work, Buzz revitalised the Company's interrogation between the contemporary and classical repertoire. Reopened in 2016 under the artistic directorship of Erica Whyman, The Other Place is once again the home for experimentation and the development of exciting new ideas.

In our 55 years of producing new plays, we have collaborated with some of the most exciting writers of their generation. These have included: Edward Albee, Howard Barker, Alice Birch, Richard Bean, Edward Bond, Howard Brenton, Marina Carr, Caryl Churchill, Martin Crimp, Can Dündar, David Edgar, Helen Edmundson, James Fenton, Georgia Fitch, Fraser Grace, David Greig, Tanika Gupta, Matt Hartley, Ella Hickson, Kirsty Housley, Dennis Kelly, Anders Lustgarten, Tarell Alvin McCraney, Martin McDonagh, Tom Morton-Smith, Rona Munro, Richard Nelson, Anthony Neilson, Harold Pinter, Phil Porter, Mike Poulton, Mark Ravenhill, Somalia Seaton, Adriano Shaplin, Tom Stoppard, debbie tucker green, Frances Ya-Chu Cowhig, Timberlake Wertenbaker, Peter Whelan and Roy Williams.

The Company today is led by Gregory Doran, whose appointment as Artistic Director represents a long-term commitment to the disciplines and craftsmanship required to put on the plays of Shakespeare. The RSC under his leadership is committed to illuminating the relevance of Shakespeare's plays and the works of his contemporaries for the next generation of audiences and believes that our continued investment in new plays and living writers is an essential part of that mission.

The RSC is grateful for the significant support of its principal funder, Arts Council England, without which our work would not be possible. Around 75 per cent of the RSC's income is self-generated from Box Office sales, sponsorship, donations, enterprise and partnerships with other organisations.

Supported using public funding by
ARTS COUNCIL ENGLAND

NEW WORK AT THE RSC

We are a contemporary theatre company built on classical rigour. Through an extensive programme of research and development, we resource writers, directors and actors to explore and develop new ideas for our stages, and as part of this we commission playwrights to engage with the muscularity and ambition of the classics and to set Shakespeare's world in the context of our own.

We invite writers to spend time with us in our rehearsal rooms, with our actors and creative teams. Alongside developing new plays for all our stages, we invite playwrights to contribute dramaturgically to both our productions of Shakespeare and his contemporaries, as well as our work for, and with, young people. We believe that engaging with living writers and contemporary theatre-makers helps to establish a creative culture within the Company which both inspires new work and creates an ever more urgent sense of enquiry into the classics.

Shakespeare was a great innovator and breaker of rules, as well as a bold commentator on the times in which he lived. It is his spirit which informs new work at the RSC. Erica Whyman, Deputy Artistic Director, heads up this strand of the Company's work alongside Pippa Hill as Literary Manager.

The work of the RSC Literary Department is generously supported by THE DRUE HEINZ TRUST.

Tartuffe was first presented by the Royal Shakespeare Company in the Swan Theatre, Stratford-upon-Avon, on 7 September 2018. The cast was as follows:

WAQAAS	**SALMAN AKHTAR**
DAMEE PERVAIZ	**RAJ BAJAJ**
AMIRA PERVAIZ	**SASHA BEHAR**
DARINA	**MICHELLE BONNARD**
ZAINAB	**SHAMIA CHALABI**
KHALIL	**JAMES CLYDE**
MARIAM PERVAIZ	**ZAINAB HASAN**
TAHIR TAUFIQ ARSUF (TARTUFFE)	**ASIF KHAN**
PC RAJ KUMAR	**NAVEED KHAN**
IMRAN PERVAIZ	**SIMON NAGRA**
PC TOM PARRY	**SAM PAY**
USMAN	**RIAD RICHIE**
DCI SARAH WELLS	**VIVIENNE SMITH**
PIPPA	**YASMIN TAHERI**
DADIMAA PERVAIZ	**AMINA ZIA**

The RSC Acting Companies are generously supported by THE GATSBY CHARITABLE FOUNDATION and THE KOVNER FOUNDATION.

Director	**Iqbal Khan**
Designer	**Bretta Gerecke**
Lighting Designer	**Richard Howell**
Composer & Music Director	**Sarah Sayeed**
Sound Designer	**Jeremy Dunn**
Movement Director	**Shelley Maxwell**
Company Voice & Text Work	**Anna McSweeney**
Assistant Director	**Nicky Cox**
Spoken Word Consultant	**Lloyd Thomas**
Casting Director	**Helena Palmer CDG**
Dramaturg	**Réjane Collard-Walker**
Production Manager	**Carl Root**
Costume Supervisor	**Sian Harris**
Props Supervisor	**Jessica Buckley**
Company Stage Manager	**Linda Fitzpatrick**
Deputy Stage Manager	**Klare Roger**
Assistant Stage Manager	**Briony Kirkman**
Producer	**Zoë Donegan**

Musicians

Vocals/Tanpura/Harmonium	**Sarah Sayeed**
Sitar/Vocals	**Pete Yelding**
Trumpet	**Andrew Stone-Fewings**
Percussion	**Joelle Barker**

This text may differ slightly from the play as performed

LOVE THE RSC?

Become a Member or Patron and support our work

The RSC is a registered charity. Our aim is to stage theatre at its best, made in Stratford-upon-Avon and shared around the world with the widest possible audience and we need your support.

Become an RSC Member from £50 per year and access up to three weeks of Priority Booking, advance information, exclusive discounts and special offers, including free on-the-day seat upgrades.

Or support as a Patron from £150 per year for up to one additional week of Priority Booking, plus enjoy opportunities to discover more through special behind-the-scenes events.

For more information visit **rsc.org.uk/support** or call the RSC Membership Office on 01789 403440.

TARTUFFE

Molière

TARTUFFE

a new version by
Anil Gupta & Richard Pinto

OBERON BOOKS
LONDON

WWW.OBERONBOOKS.COM

First published in 2018 by Oberon Books Ltd
521 Caledonian Road, London N7 9RH
Tel: +44 (0) 20 7607 3637 / Fax: +44 (0) 20 7607 3629
e-mail: info@oberonbooks.com
www.oberonbooks.com

PB ISBN: 9781786826237
E ISBN: 9781786826398

Cover photography by Paul Stuart © RSC

Printed and bound by 4EDGE Limited, Hockley, Essex, UK.
eBook conversion by Lapiz Digital Services, India.

A few words of thanks to some people who have been instrumental in getting this particular version of a classic play into print...

to Greg Doran, for kicking it all off;
to Réjane Collard-Walker, for her invaluable support and advice;
to Iqbal Khan, for his tireless enthusiasm and inventiveness;
and to Lloyd Thomas for his explosive lyrical contribution.

ACT I

SCENE 1

The open plan living/dining room of a large executive style home in an affluent suburb of Birmingham. It's home to a British Pakistani Muslim family – the Parvaizes.

There is a large glass and chrome dining table and chairs. A large leather sofa and armchair around an 'ethnic' coffee table. There are double doors leading out to the hall, and another door to a downstairs loo.

Music is playing over bluetooth speakers in the corner of the room (the whole house is wired for sound). It's Black Sabbath's 'Sweet Leaf'.

After a couple of beats, DARINA, 40s, Bosnian with dyed yellow blonde hair, a tight white shirt and leggings, bursts out from the downstairs loo. She has Marigolds on and is carrying a bucket of cleaning stuff and holding a loo brush as if it's a mic. She has her eyes tightly closed and is singing along loudly to the music. After a few seconds she opens her eyes and notices the audience.

DARINA: Oh!

> *(Shouting.)* Sorry! I didn't know you were… *(She turns off the music.)* Sorry. I like to have music when I am… *(She mimes cleaning the loo with the loo brush.)* Cleaning the toilet!

> *(To audience member.)* You like Black Sabbath? I do. Very big band in Bosnia when I was a girl. We like rock music in Bosnia. I am Bosnian. Dobra Dan.

> *(Beat.)* Means hello.

> Lot of cleaners don't do that. I always do. And I pull the fridge out and hoover behind. That's why the Pervaiz family keep me on.

A beat.

(To 'stupid' audience member.) I am cleaner. This is their house – the Pervaizes. Very nice family, you know. Live in very nice part of Birmingham, yes there nice parts in Birmingham. Originally from Pakistan, but now also very English. You know how I know? Always tidy the house before I come.

More than ten years now. They are good to me. And I sort out family mess, straighten things out and help with dirty laundry. So not just a cleaner, eh?

She starts plumping the cushions on the sofa.

Also, you should know, they are Muslims. It's OK. Don't be scared. I am Muslim too. You didn't know Bosnians were Muslim? What they teach you in school?

We hear sounds of people approaching.

They're coming. Don't worry. Apart from being immigrants, and brown, and Muslim, they're perfectly normal. Just like *(looks at audience)* well, some of you.

DADIMAA (OOV): *(Punjabi.)* Go, quick, and get my coat! *(English.)* I want to leave before the traffic picks up.

The family traipse in. DADIMAA PERVAIZ is leaving. AMIRA, her daughter-in-law, MARIAM, her granddaughter, NADEEM (DAMEE) her grandson, and KHALIL (formerly Colin, white Muslim convert, friend of family, IMRAN's accountant) are all scurrying around her. PIPPA, her brow-beaten care worker, stays by the doorway.

AMIRA: Why are you going so soon? Stay for dinner.

DADIMAA: Who's cooking?

AMIRA: I am.

DADIMAA: No thank you.

AMIRA: Dadimaa…

DADIMAA: Dadimaa chachi… No need to be polite… I know *you* don't want me here.

AMIRA: We love having you here…

DAMEE comes over with her coat.

DAMEE: Here's your coat, Dadimaa.

DADIMAA: See! They can't wait for me to leave.

DAMEE: You told me to get your coat…

DADIMAA: Stop arguing with me and show some respect for once!

AMIRA: Please, Maaji. Stay and eat with us.

DADIMAA: I told you I'm not hungry! *(Punjabi.)* I'm not hungry!

AMIRA: We're having your favourite. Lamb.

DADIMAA: What do you know what's my favourite, huh? *(To the others.)* She's been in this family two minutes and she knows my favourite… *(To AMIRA.)* Too much red meat is bad for me *(To the others.)* It's probably not even halal…

AMIRA: I could do chicken instead?

DADIMAA: Salmonella! She wants to kill me. *(Punjabi.)* Can you believe this woman?

AMIRA: *(To DARINA.)* I think there's some vegetarian curry in the…

DADIMAA: What am I, a Hindu now?

DARINA joins in.

3

DARINA: Please, Mrs Parvaiz, I'm sure that we can find something…

DADIMAA: I don't think we need to hear from the servants…

MARIAM: Dadimaa, you can't talk to Darina like that. Women need to be respected in their working environment and their voices should be heard!

DADIMAA: No sound should be coming from her, except sound of hoover!

MARIAM: Well that's not my truth. Besides, Darina is like one of the family…

DADIMAA: Really? Does she look like family? *(To DARINA.)* My son pays you to clean, not talk. Get your mop. Downstairs toilet has blockage.

DAMEE: *(To MARIAM.)* Wonder who did that.

MARIAM tries to suppress her laughter. DADIMAA sees her.

DADIMAA: *(To MARIAM.)* Be careful, beti. You think because you're clever girl, been to university, you can do what you want? Well I'm not stupid. You think this hair turned white from sitting in the sun? And I won't let you bring shame on this family. Trust me.

MARIAM shakes her head. AMIRA puts a reassuring hand on MARIAM's arm. MARIAM ignores it.

(Punjabi.) I know what these girls get up to. Acting like sluts…

DAMEE: Dadimaa, don't be cussing on her like that, man, what's wrong with you?

DADIMAA: And this one…thinks he is some kala gora gangsta rapper.

DAMEE: Here we go.

DADIMAA: I know you're my grandson and a boy and therefore more important than your sister, but still. Befakoof.

AMIRA gives DAMEE a reassuring look.

AMIRA: She doesn't mean it.

DAMEE kisses his teeth and blanks AMIRA. KAHLIL, IMRAN's timid accountant, feels compelled to step in.

KHALIL: *(Coughs.)* Mrs Pervaiz, if you'll forgive me, I do think you might be overreacting just a little bit.

DADIMAA: Khalilji, you are my son's accountant, and old friend of family, and you have also converted to Islam, and that's why we have to be nice to you. But you're not family, so this is none of your business *(Punjabi.)* so keep your little dunda out of it! *(English, turning to the others.)* I'm sorry to be blunt, but I have to speak my mind, even if it means I upset people.

AMIRA: Nobody's upset with you, maaji…

DADIMAA: And nobody asked you for your opinion. *(To the others.)* Disrespect wherever I look. At least now we have someone in the house who know how to behave like a good Muslim should behave, praise be to Allah.

DAMEE: You don't mean Tartuffe?

DADIMAA: Call him by his proper name, dummy! Not Tartuffe, he is Tahir Taufiq Arsuf! And he is a holy man.

DAMEE: He's not a holy man!

DADIMAA: He is a holy man! He walks the righteous path!

DAMEE: What, hanging round people's houses, leeching off dem, using their PS4 like he owns it.

DADIMAA: My son has never made a wiser decision in his life than to bring that man into his home. Allah himself has sent him to you!

DAMEE: The guy's a creep. I swear, if he carries on messing with dad's head like he has been… *(Flexes his muscles.)* Man gwan get mash up big style. Pardon my French…

DARINA: *(To DAMEE.)* I don't think that's French.

DADIMAA: You should listen to him. All of you. He knows so much. He's told me. Turreya te appareya. There's so much he can teach you.

DARINA: In Bosnia we have a saying, 'Where people are promising much to you, bring a small bag.'

They all look puzzled. A beat.

DADIMAA: Where *is* my bag?

MARIAM hurriedly gets her handbag for her.

Mark my words. Follow the word of Allah, like Tahir Arsuf, or you'll all end up burning in hell, burning to a crisp.

DAMEE smirks and rolls his eyes.

Oh, you think it's funny that you're all going to hell?

DAMEE shakes his head. AMIRA steps in.

AMIRA: Really, Maaji, you shouldn't be too hard on them. They're good kids.

DADIMAA turns on her.

DADIMAA: I don't need you telling me about my own grandchildren, thank you. They're my blood, not yours! This family…it used to be so strong. A proper Pakistani Muslim family. Their mother, Allah protect her spirit, *(Punjabi)* she was an angel, a wonderful mother *(English)* and a credit to Muslim women the world over. Then she passed, and what were they left with? A cleaner instead of a mother. And I thought it couldn't get any worse. And then…you came along.

AMIRA is lost for words. She turns to MARIAM and DAMEE for support, but gets none.

Still, my son has made his choice. And you got what you wanted. But I won't stay in this house a moment longer. And I will never eat food from the hand of this Kanjri!

AMIRA is dumbstruck. DARINA puts a supportive hand on her arm. DADIMAA picks up some burfi from a dish on a dresser in the hall on her way out.

I'll take a couple of these sweeties for the journey.

MARIAM: What about your diabetes?

DADIMAA: Tahir Arsuf says I don't have diabetes.

DAMEE: He's a doctor now as well, is he?

DADIMAA: *(Full of admiration.)* Oh, he's many, many things.

She pokes PIPPA, her care worker.

Come on! What are you waiting for? You're supposed to be looking after me, I'm very old and frail and I can't take care of myself.

They all leave to show DADIMAA out at the door, apart from KHALIL and DARINA.

7

KHALIL: I'll just wait here 'til she's…

DARINA: Yes.

KHALIL: She's a feisty old lady.

DARINA: Don't let her hear you call her old.

KHALIL: Ha!

KHALIL nervously looks back into the hall to see if she heard.

Very complicated, isn't it? All this?

DARINA: All what?

KHALIL: Pakistani family relationships. Difficult to grasp all
the nuances. I'm from Kidderminster, you see.

DARINA: Don't you have families in Kidderminster?

KHALIL: Why is she so obsessed with this Tartuffe bloke
anyway?

DARINA: That is nothing compared to Mr Parvaiz. He's ten
times worse.

KHALIL: Imran? Why, what's he doing?

DARINA: Is like he's in love with the guy. *(Off KHALIL's look.)*
Not actually in love. It's like bromance. Like George
Clooney and Brad Pitt – if George Clooney and Brad Pitt
were Pakistani. And Muslim. He tells him all his secrets,
lets him tell him what to do. And he's always give him
things. Give him anything he want. Other day he gave
him the last chocolate hobnob? I noticed that.

KHALIL: Clever.

DARINA: I notice lots of little things like that.

KHALIL: You should be a detective.

DARINA: Oh, thank you!

KHALIL: *(To himself.)* Cos you certainly don't seem to do any cleaning...

DARINA: *(Not listening.)* If this Tartuffe farts, Imran is sniffing it to make sure he's OK. He's a superhero to Imran – like Iron Man and Thor, rolled into one, but without the nice muscles.

She thinks about Thor's muscles for a moment.

KHALIL: Well, when you've had as much experience in the world of business as I have, you get a pretty good feel for people.

DARINA rolls her eyes. KHALIL is about to pontificate again.

I like to think that, in my own little way, because I'm a good judge of character, and because I've had a reasonable amount of business success in this area...

DARINA starts hoovering around KHALIL.

DARINA: Do you mind?

KHALIL: No, you go ahead... I can see a little deeper into the psyche of the British Pakistani. And I have to say I'm beginning to think that, if as you suggest, this Tartuffe isn't quite 'pukka', to borrow from the vernacular of the subcontinent! Mm?

He chuckles to himself.

DARINA: *(To audience.)* What a knob.

KHALIL: Which is a bit of a worry, considering the amount of cash coming out of Imran's bank account.

DARINA turns the hoover off.

DARINA: Woah, woah, woah...

KHALIL: Hmm?

DARINA: What did you say about bank account?

KHALIL: I was just making the observation that there's been
some unusual activity on his account – not that I'm
suggesting there might be anything untoward happening.
But I have to say that as his accountant I have to say I'm
very worried. Obviously I'm also very worried as his
Muslim brother. And his friend. I'm very worried as his
friend. Probably friend first, then accountant, then...

DARINA: I get it.

KHALIL: *(Joking.)* Maybe that's this Tartuffe guy's plan, to save
Imran from damnation by relieving him of all his money
and worldly possessions!

DARINA: This is not good.

KHALIL: No, it isn't.

DARINA: Something needs to be done about this man.

KHALIL: Yes. Although as an accountant I would always
advise against drastic action. In fact, any kind of action...

DARINA: This man is great big pain in guzica.

AMIRA and DAMEE come back in.

SCENE 3

AMIRA: *(To KHALIL.)* You dodged a bullet there.

KHALIL smiles. DAMEE looks at AMIRA.

DAMEE: She's your mother-in-law.

AMIRA: I wasn't being disrespectful.

DAMEE: I'm just saying.

A beat of tension in the air.

DARINA: Who wants cup of tea?

AMIRA: No thanks, Darina. I can feel another migraine coming on. I think I heard Imran's Mercedes in the drive, tell him I've gone for a lie down before dinner.

She heads upstairs.

KHALIL: I'll just say a quick hello before I shoot off.

DARINA: *(Aside to audience.)* He's never said quick hello in his life.

DARINA leaves.

SCENE 4

DAMEE: Khalil, could you have a word with Dad about Mariam and Waqaas?

KHALIL: What about them?

DAMEE: I reckon Tartuffe's against them getting married. He's trying to get Dad to stop it.

KHALIL: Really?

DAMEE: I mean, it's well out of order them interfering in that relationship. My sister's happiness is the most important thing in the world to me. I can't stand by and let them destroy it. And, you know, not that this is anything to do with it or nothing, but I'm sort of seeing Waqaas's sister, Zainab. She's my life, guy, my jaan, my rani, my everything...

DARINA: He's coming!

DAMEE: So if him and Mariam get married, I'll be well in with his mum and dad you know what I'm talking about cuz?

DAMEE leaves.

SCENE 5

IMRAN enters. He's late 40s, full of himself, self-made 'arriviste', bouncing in with great energy and confidence.

IMRAN: Salaam aleikum, salaam aleikum…

ALL: Waleikum assalaam.

IMRAN: How's things?

KHALIL: I was just leaving, but it's lucky I've bumped into you because I wanted to have a quick word…

IMRAN: Well, that's not going to happen, is it? 'Quick word'? You? Eh?

He looks round at the others for appreciation of his 'joke' – he's bombastic, likes being in charge.

DARINA: *(To audience.)* I've already done that one.

IMRAN slaps KHALIL on the back and moves on.

IMRAN: Darina…

KHALIL: It's about…

IMRAN: Hold on, buddy, I just want to catch up with the family *(To DARINA.)* Have I missed anything while I've been away? Everyone ok?

DARINA: Well, your wife's had a raging migraine for two days solid.

IMRAN: Right. And how's Tartuffeji?

DARINA: Tartuffe? He's alright.

IMRAN: Only alright? That doesn't sound good.

DARINA: Amira's hardly eaten, her headache was that bad.

IMRAN: And what about Tartuffeji, what did he eat?

DARINA: So far today he's had breakfast, lunch and now a
huge bowl of chicken curry in front of TV in your study.

IMRAN: Why do you let him eat on his own? Poor guy, he'll
be feeling lonely.

DARINA presses on with trying to bring the attention back to AMIRA.

DARINA: I think you need to get Amira to speak to GP. She
should see neurologist.

IMRAN nods.

IMRAN: Mm. Mm. And how about Tartuffeji?

DARINA: He is not neurologist.

IMRAN: No, but he doesn't feel like he's been neglected. I
wouldn't want him to think we'd forgotten about him.

DARINA: He doesn't think that.

IMRAN: Oh thank God for that.

DARINA: Yeah, so they're both fine, that's good isn't it? I'll go
and tell your wife how pleased you are that she's still alive.

*She goes out, leaving KHALIL and IMRAN alone. IMRAN sits at the
table and starts looking at some paperwork.*

KHALIL: You do know that she's ever so slightly taking the
mickey out of you, don't you?

A beat. IMRAN looks to the doorway.

IMRAN: Really?

KHALIL: Yes. And I have to say, although I don't want to upset you or criticise you in any way, I have to say that she may have a point.

IMRAN: What do you mean?

KHALIL is nervous about confronting IMRAN but screws his courage to the sticking place.

KHALIL: *(Clears throat.)* This business with Tartuffe. I mean, you've dragged him in off the street, and it seems perhaps like you've almost given him the run of your home...

IMRAN is collecting up his paperwork.

IMRAN: Woah, woah, woah, woah. Hold on a minute.

He gets up and puts his paperwork in his briefcase.

Don't start having a pop at Tartuffeji. You don't even know the man.

KHALIL: Look, OK, granted, I haven't known him as long as you have, but I've known him long enough to see that he appears to be taking you for a ride.

IMRAN: 'Taking me for a ride'?

KHALIL: Not 'taking you for a ride' as such, but it's just, you know – you seem to be in his thrall. You don't seem to listen to anyone else these [days]...

IMRAN's not listening, cuts in.

IMRAN: Ah, Khalil, mate, if you had known him as long as I have... I tell you, you'd really like him. You would, you'd be blown away. I mean, this is a guy who...he's just...oh, you know...if you listen to him for just a few minutes, the whole world suddenly makes perfect sense, you know what I mean? And then everything else is just unimportant. He's completely turned my life around. Do you know what I realised, Khalil. Up until now, I was going nowhere. My life had no meaning. Yes, I had the house, and the events business, and the Mercedes, and the Norwegian spruce decking on the patio that cost seven thousand pounds, but was I happy?

KHALIL: Yes?

IMRAN: No! But that man, that angel, has set me on the right path. The path of truth.

KHALIL: Really.

IMRAN: Really. Don't forget, brother, we're Muslims. Do you know what that means.

KHALIL: I think so.

IMRAN: No you don't. You think you do because you're new to it. But we've lost sight of what true Islam is all about. It's been westernised. Assimilated. To find our true Muslim selves we need to cast off the shackles of this empty consumer society. We must rise up above materialism and banish all thoughts of worldly possessions.

KHALIL: Even Norwegian spruce decking?

IMRAN misses the sarcasm.

IMRAN: *(Having an evangelical 'hallelujah' moment.)* Even the decking! Alhamdulillah! Do you want to know how far this wonderful man has brought me? I have become so freed from worldly cares, so removed from the trappings of this world, so *righteous* deep in my soul, that if I lost my entire family tomorrow in a terrible accident, I wouldn't be sad. In fact, it wouldn't bother me at all, because I know one day I'll see them again in a better place.

KHALIL: Wow. That is righteous.

IMRAN: I remember, when I first saw Tartuffeji at the mosque…he was kneeling opposite me, and praying so intensely – throwing his arms up, sighing and moaning so loudly – that everyone stopped their own prayers and turned to watch him. He was clearly the closest one to Allah in that room.

KHALIL: Right. Because the most religious people are the ones that moan the most?

IMRAN: *(Over his head again.)* Exactly. And as I left the mosque he ran in front of me to give me a blessing. I found out who he was, and everyone said how poor and holy he was, so I gave him some money. But would he take it?

KHALIL: Yes?

IMRAN: No, not all of it. *(A beat.)* He insisted on giving half of it back.

KHALIL: What a trooper.

IMRAN: I know. And the half he kept, he went straight off and gave it to the poor. Every time I went to the mosque we'd go through the same routine – prayers, moaning, blessing; prayers, moaning, blessing… Prayers…

KHALIL: …moaning, blessing. I get it.

IMRAN: Eventually I thought, this guy is the real deal. So I decided, or *Allah* decided, to take him in and give him somewhere to stay.

KHALIL is nodding.

And the moment he set foot in this house, is the moment when we started living as real Muslims at last. He keeps me away from any bad influences – television, newspapers…

KHALIL: Friends…

IMRAN: All of that. And it's not just me. He's trying to help the whole family. He's taken a real interest in Amira. Wants to know what she's doing, where she's going, keeps an eye on what she's wearing. He's more jealous of her than I am! He's really looking out for me, there. What do you think? You think he's an angel?

KHALIL: I really wouldn't know.

IMRAN: I think he might be.

KHALIL: Probably not.

IMRAN: Oh?

KHALIL: I'm just saying, it's unlikely. I mean, would a real angel keep going on about how angelic he was? I mean, isn't it more angelic to not make such a big deal about it?

IMRAN: I'm not with you.

KHALIL: If he says material things are so bad what's he doing up in your study, in your silk dressing gown in front of your fifty-inch plasma telly.

IMRAN: He's taking my burden from me.

KHALIL: Or maybe what he's taking from you is your kids' inheritance, and possibly salting it away in some untraceable and definitely un-Islamic offshore bank account.

IMRAN: OK, that's enough. *(A beat.)* Yes, you're an accountant and you know a lot about deductible capital expenditure – Allah knows I've had to listen to chapter and verse on that subject…

KHALIL: It's a very important part of UK tax law…

IMRAN: But what we're talking about here is a bit more profound. This is about being a Muslim, about the Qur'an, about the true word of Allah, about man's eternal soul. So you stick to your spreadsheets and let Tartuffeji worry about that.

KHALIL: Look, I haven't got all the answers…

IMRAN: You've kept that quiet.

KHALIL: And whilst I would never doubt the sincerity of any true believers, I mean I am one myself, there are some people who use religion to lead people astray, and you know, maybe, *maybe* Tartuffe is one of those guys. And maybe there's like, a 'cultural' connection between you and him that makes it harder for you to see what he really is.

IMRAN: A cultural connection?

KHALIL: *(Off IMRAN's look.)* Or maybe not.

IMRAN nods. A beat.

IMRAN: Are we done?

Another beat.

KHALIL: I think so.

IMRAN starts to go.

Oh, actually there was just one other thing.

IMRAN sighs.

IMRAN: Really?

KHALIL: It's about Waqaas and Mariam.

IMRAN: Oh, not that again…

KHALIL: The wedding date was set, venue booked and then you cancelled it.

IMRAN: I don't want to talk about it.

KHALIL: But why? They're good kids, they love each other, what's the problem?

IMRAN: I don't want to talk about it! *(A beat, then pointedly.)* It's a cultural thing.

ACT II

SCENE 1

Bedroom/study. MARIAM is alone, on the sofa with her laptop. She's a bookish type, fresh from university. She's playing her iTunes playlist on the bluetooth speakers – gentle, student-indie-band-type music. IMRAN enters.

IMRAN: Hello Mariam, beti.

MARIAM: Hi Dad!

IMRAN: What are doing? Snapchatting your mates? Or watching some cutesy cat videos on YouTube?

MARIAM: I'm reading about how mobile phone technology is economically empowering women in Sub-Saharan Africa.

IMRAN: Achaa.

MARIAM: It's actually really important. It might even start to impact the Global Gender Pay Gap Index…

IMRAN: *(Not really listening.)* Mmmm, mmm…

He stands awkwardly for a moment.

So, I wanted to talk to you about something…

MARIAM: OK.

IMRAN: It's nothing to worry about…

He opens the door to the hall and the door to the loo to check there's no one there.

MARIAM: What are you doing?

IMRAN: Just checking no one's about.

MARIAM: Now I'm worried.

IMRAN: Don't be silly beti. It's all perfectly fine.

He sits down next to her.

Right, there we go! This is cosy isn't it?

MARIAM: *(Puzzled.)* Yeah.

IMRAN: I like your music!

MARIAM: Thanks.

IMRAN: Shall we turn it off?

MARIAM turns it off.

So, beti, here's the thing…you know you're my favourite daughter?

MARIAM: I'm you're only daughter.

She smiles. It's their little joke.

IMRAN: Yeah. But you've always been such a lovely girl. So sweet, so kind, so…considerate. That's why I love you so much…

MARIAM: Oh. Thanks.

IMRAN: You don't need to thank me… My point is that you always seem to want to make me happy. Is that true?

MARIAM: *(Where's this going?)* Well, obviously I want you to be happy…

IMRAN: Great. See? This is easy, isn't it?

MARIAM nods, unsure. A beat. MARIAM goes back to her laptop. IMRAN gets up and takes a few steps away, pretends to examine a pot plant.

(Casual.) What do you think of Tartuffeji?

MARIAM: Hmm?

IMRAN: Tartuffeji. What do you think of him?

MARIAM: Me?

IMRAN: Yes.

MARIAM: What do I think of him?

IMRAN: Yes.

MARIAM: He's alright.

IMRAN: Yeah. He is, isn't he? And he's got this incredible mind, hasn't he? He knows so much about Islam. And there's like this aura about him, you know, like a kind of spirituality that seems to flow over you whenever you're around him, don't you think?

A beat.

MARIAM: He's alright.

IMRAN: So you like him?

MARIAM: I suppose. If you do.

IMRAN: Good. Good answer! You're a good girl.

MARIAM: Thanks.

IMRAN: You don't need to keep saying thanks. So you think he's a good guy then…

MARIAM: I suppose so.

IMRAN: He's got a good heart. Very caring.

MARIAM: Uh huh.

IMRAN: So you wouldn't be averse to seeing more of him. Spending a bit more time with him. Maybe as his wife.

MARIAM: Sure…wait, what?

IMRAN: What do you think? Is it a 'yes' from you?

MARIAM: What did you just say?

IMRAN: When?

MARIAM: I think I must have misheard you.

IMRAN: Did you?

MARIAM: What did you say after 'spend more time with him'?

IMRAN: *(Trying to remember.)* Um...

MARIAM: Because it sounded like 'as his wife'.

IMRAN: That was it.

MARIAM: You're not serious?

IMRAN: What do you mean? You want to get married don't you?

MARIAM: Yes, to Waqaas...

He holds a hand up to cut her off.

IMRAN: And it would make me very happy.

MARIAM: OK. But, erm, shouldn't I be able to choose my own husband?

IMRAN: Of course. But I am your father and I'm giving you a shortlist. Of one.

MARIAM: Stop being weird, Dad.

IMRAN: I'm not being weird.

MARIAM: You always told me you wanted me to chase my dreams. Get an education. Go to university. Be a strong, independent woman.

IMRAN: Exactly. I told you to do that, and you did it. Good girl. And now I'm telling you to do this.

MARIAM: Dad…

IMRAN: I've made my mind up, Mariam. This family has to get back on the right track, on Allah's track, and that means Tartuffeji needs to be one of us. If he's going to save us he has to be with us every day. He has to be part of this family. And the only way he can be part of this family is if he marries you.

MARIAM looks at him. He's got to be nuts.

MARIAM: This isn't you.

IMRAN: What?

MARIAM: I don't understand why you're trying to be someone you're not.

IMRAN: This is who I am. This is who I've always been.

MARIAM: Maybe you've been working too hard or something…

IMRAN: Because I've rediscovered my faith? You think Islam is a stress-related illness?

MARIAM: But this isn't your faith, this is just wrong!

IMRAN: You see, you saying that only proves how much you need to be saved.

MARIAM: Okay, maybe, you know, for whatever reason you've started to feel differently about things…

IMRAN: Mariam, this is…

MARIAM: But why don't we talk about that?

IMRAN: This is the right…

MARIAM: Maybe we could find another way to…

IMRAN: *(Shouting.)* THIS IS THE RIGHT THING TO DO! Stop thinking about yourself for one minute and just… just look at the bigger picture! *(A beat.)* This isn't about me making decisions for you any more. This is about Allah making decisions. And he doesn't make mistakes like we do. Like I do. He always does the right thing.

A pause. IMRAN sits next to MARIAM again.

Listen to me. You might not see it yet, but this man is a good man, and I know you'll be happy with him. *(A beat.)* A long time ago I promised… I promised your mother I would take care of you. How can I keep that promise if I allow you to turn away from Allah?

A pause. MARIAM is in shock. Suddenly there is a loud clattering noise from behind the curtains – like a bucket being dropped. IMRAN gets up, goes over and pulls back the curtains. DARINA is there. A beat. She reaches down and picks up the bucket and holds up her duster.

What are you doing?

DARINA: I clean curtains, I have not hear a single word.

IMRAN: Really?

DARINA: I swear it!

IMRAN: *(Satisfied.)* Okay, good…

IMRAN turns and goes back to MARIAM. DARINA hurries after him.

DARINA: But promise me you are not actually make her marry him are you?

IMRAN: What?

DARINA: I mean, is joke yes? Not even you would do such stupid thing.

IMRAN: It's not a joke.

DARINA: Yes, is joke. Very good! Very funny winding up for all of us, ha ha!

IMRAN: I am deadly serious.

DARINA: Yeah, of course. And I am Queen of England. *(Impersonating Queen.)* 'How do you do, Muslim peoples!'

IMRAN: *(To DARINA.)* Can I speak to my daughter?

DARINA: She's not listen anymore, fun is over, let's talk something else.

IMRAN: *(To MARIAM.)* You see, marrying Tartuffe will…

DARINA: *(To MARIAM.)* Ignore him, he's taking piss!

IMRAN: *(Angry.)* In the name of Allah, let me speak!

A beat.

DARINA: Okay, so you're not joking. And shame on you for that. How can you be so crazy that…

IMRAN: Enough! This is none of your business. And I won't have some 'chuurie' taking to me like that.

DARINA: Then you fire me.

IMRAN thinks better of it.

(Nodding.) Yeah, maybe not.

IMRAN: Just keep out of it, okay?

DARINA: Fine.

IMRAN: Thank you.

DARINA: I won't say anything.

IMRAN: Great.

DARINA: I just think it.

IMRAN glares at her. He decides to leave it for now.

IMRAN: *(To MARIAM.)* I'll talk to you later, when we're alone. *(To DARINA.)* You missed a bit.

He points to the curtains, then goes out.

SCENE 2

DARINA: What is matter with you? You not say nothing, I have to speak for you – and if I have to speak for you is take long time, cos I have enough trouble speaking for me.

MARIAM: He is my father, Darina.

DARINA: This is not medieval times, *moja draga.* You are the one who must be happy in marriage, not father. Tell him if he likes Tartuffe so much, he can marry the guy himself.

MARIAM shakes her head.

MARIAM: You don't understand...

DARINA: Look, Waqaas wants to marry you, right?

MARIAM nods.

And you want to marry him, yes?

MARIAM nods.

So what is problem? You love him, don't you?

MARIAM: More than anything in the whole world.

DARINA: And he loves you?

MARIAM: Yes, of course he does.

DARINA: So you can't Tartuffe. Because you want to Waqaas.

MARIAM: I know.

DARINA: Good. It's better when you take father out of equation. Then is right, is normal way for people to get together.

MARIAM: Well, I don't think 'normal' is the right word when there are so many alternatives to heteronormative socio-sexual constructs…

DARINA: You know what I mean!

MARIAM: Yes, I do…

A beat.

DARINA: Good. So. What are you going to do about it?

She thinks about it, then comes up with an answer.

MARIAM: Kill myself.

DARINA: Brilliant. Why didn't I think of that? Completely sorted…

MARIAM nods.

(Turning on her.) What are you talking about, you idiot!

MARIAM is startled.

MARIAM: Darina!

DARINA: 'Oh, no, everything is terrible, I can't do anything…' I can't stand if peoples are so stupid.

MARIAM: I'm not stupid. I'm just…not very brave, that's all.

DARINA: Love must make you brave, otherwise what is it worth?

28

MARIAM: Why can't Waqaas be brave! It's a man thing, isn't it?

DARINA looks at her.

DARINA: 'A man thing'?

MARIAM: *(Feebly.)* Isn't it Waqaas' job to persuade dad to let us get married?

DARINA: It's not Waqaas' fault your father is go crazy. You have to tell him you don't want to marry Tartuffe.

MARIAM: I can't. I don't know what to say.

DARINA: No?

MARIAM: It's not that easy.

DARINA: What they teach you at your university?

MARIAM: I read Women's Studies. *(Beat.)* Examining gender as a social and cultural construct and the relationship between power and gender.

DARINA: And that mean do whatever your father say?

MARIAM: I don't know! The course is about women in Sub-Saharan Africa, not bloody Birmingham!

DARINA shakes her head.

Maybe he'll change his mind. And Tartuffe probably won't want to marry me anyway.

DARINA: You know what? You are right. Don't make fuss. Let men sort everything out for you.

MARIAM: I didn't mean…

DARINA: Yes, much better for womens not think about anything. Just do as we are told, wear burqa, don't drive car, marry creepy old guy…

MARIAM: Oh God. You have to help me get out of it.

DARINA: No, daughter must obey father, even if he tells her to marry monkey. I'm sure you will be very happy, cooking for him, cleaning for him, shaving his hairy back…

MARIAM: I mean it. Please. I'll do anything.

DARINA: No, really, this is the happiness you deserve.

MARIAM: If I tell dad I'm in love with Waqaas…

DARINA: Too late. This time next month you will be married with this man, and he will be giving you a proper 'Tartuffing'!

MARIAM: Fine. If you won't help me I'll deal with it alone.

A beat. MARIAM considers her options. She has an idea.

I know. I'm going to…

MARIAM/DARINA: …kill myself/yourself.

DARINA: Come on, is okay. I find way for you. *(Sees something out of the window.)* Oh, great.

MARIAM: What is it?

DARINA: Your boyfriend's here.

MARIAM: Tartuffe!

DARINA: No! Boyfriend! The one you like.

MARIAM: Waqaas! *(To DARINA.)* That's good isn't it?

DARINA: Old Bosnian saying… 'Only one bad thing about having *right end* of the stick: *wrong end* is free for someone else to grab hold of.'

WAQAAS enters. He's an earnest, bright, bookish young man. Not very eloquent or socially confident. He stands by the door, clearly in a highly emotional state, but not sure what to say. DARINA and MARIAM stare at him, expectantly. A beat. He goes to say something but can't. Another beat. He tries again and fails again. DARINA loses patience.

What!

WAQAAS: *(Dramatically.)* Is it true!?

DARINA: You are asking me?

WAQAAS: No, sorry. Mariam.

MARIAM: What?

WAQAAS: Is it true?

MARIAM: Is what true?

WAQAAS: What they're saying at the mosque.

A beat.

MARIAM: What are they saying at the mosque?

WAQAAS: That…you're going to get married to this Tartuffe bloke.

MARIAM: They're saying that at the mosque!

WAQAAS: Yeah!

MARIAM: Oh God!

WAQAAS: I know. Imagine how that made me feel?

MARIAM: How it made you feel?

WAQAAS: Yeah. They looked at me like I was a right idiot.

DARINA: I know what they mean.

MARIAM: Sorry, so what is it that you wanted?

WAQAAS: Are you planning to marry Tartuffe?

MARIAM: It's my dad's idea. I didn't know he'd told anyone else.

WAQAAS: Right. So you are?

MARIAM: Did I say that?

WAQAAS: Mariam, please, just tell me what's going on. I think I have a right to know.

MARIAM: You have a right? What about my rights?

WAQAAS: I'm not with you.

MARIAM: That is so typical.

WAQAAS: Are you going to marry Tartuffe or not!

MARIAM: What do you think?

WAQAAS: What do I think?

MARIAM: Yes.

WAQAAS: I think you should. If that's what you all want.

MARIAM: And that's your advice, is it?

WAQAAS: Yup. I'm sure you'll be very happy together.

MARIAM: Thanks.

WAQAAS: You're welcome.

DARINA has opened a bag of sweets, settled into a comfy chair to enjoy the show. She puts her feet up.

DARINA: *(To audience.)* When you are in love, your heart is very big, but your brain is very small…

WAQAAS: *(To MARIAM.)* So, is that it then?

MARIAM: Looks like it.

WAQAAS: And all that stuff you said, about being in love with me…

MARIAM: Well you just said I should marry whoever my dad chooses for me, so…

WAQAAS: Don't make this all out to be my fault. This is just an excuse to dump me. To get out of your promise. Well next time just send me a text.

MARIAM: There won't be a next time.

WAQAAS: Good. And you know what? I actually think you probably never liked me at all.

MARIAM: You can think what you want.

WAQAAS: I can think what I want.

MARIAM: I know.

WAQAAS: And don't worry about me. I'll be fine.

MARIAM: I'm sure.

WAQAAS: There's a lot of other girls interested in me, actually.

MARIAM: What, on Geek to Geek dot com?

WAQAAS: No! Not just that one.

MARIAM: So who are all these other women?

WAQAAS: Who are they?

MARIAM: Yeah.

A beat.

WAQAAS: You mean what are their names?

MARIAM nods.

Well, there's…and… Look, I'm not going to go through
them all.

MARIAM: I thought that was the idea.

WAQAAS: Well I've got to move on, haven't I? You can't
expect me to hang around here, watching you with…him.

MARIAM: But you are though, aren't you?

WAQAAS: What?

MARIAM: Hanging around.

WAQAAS: You want me to go?

MARIAM shrugs.

Fine, I'm going. *(He turns to leave.)*

MARIAM: Bye.

He comes back.

WAQAAS: And you know that playlist I made you? I want you
to delete it. From all your devices. And the iCloud.

He turns to leave again.

MARIAM: I will.

He comes back.

WAQAAS: Remember, this was your idea.

MARIAM: Okay.

WAQAAS: I'm just going along with it.

MARIAM: Good.

WAQAAS: Right, this is it. I'm going.

He goes to the door.

MARIAM: So you said.

He turns back at the door.

WAQAAS: I won't be coming back.

MARIAM: Uh-huh.

WAQAAS: Right…

He puts his hand on the door to turn the handle but turns back again.

MARIAM/WAQAAS: What?

WAQAAS: I thought you said something.

MARIAM: *(Shaking her head.)* Not me.

WAQAAS: Right. Right. I'm going, then. Goodbye.

He walks slowly away, glancing back surreptitiously to see if she's trying to stop him.

MARIAM: Goodbye!

DARINA: Oh for goodness' sake! *(She jumps up and grabs WAQAAS by the arm.)* Come down!

WAQAAS: No! It's no use trying to stop me!

MARIAM: If he's staying I'm going!

She starts to leave, DARINA lets go of WAQAAS and grabs MARIAM instead.

DARINA: Hey, you stay here!

MARIAM: It's too late, Darina. We're finished!

WAQAAS: Goodbye, Mariam!

DARINA: How many times you going to say goodbye and not go anywhere?

DARINA, keeping hold of MARIAM, retrieves WAQAAS and drags them both back to the centre of the stage.

WAQAAS: What are you doing?

MARIAM: Yes, what are you doing?

DARINA: I am make everything ok between you.

WAQAAS: Were you not listening? She's not interested.

MARIAM: He doesn't care about me.

DARINA: He loves you and you love him, and you both know this, in the name of Allah give us all a break and shut the bloody hells up! *(She puts their hands together.)* Just say 'I love you' and have big kiss and that's that.

They hold hands without looking at each other. WAQAAS turns to her at last.

WAQAAS: We can't kiss unless we're facing the same way.

MARIAM smiles, looks sideways at him.

Why did you say those things about me?

MARIAM: Why did you say those things about *me*...?

DARINA: *(Interrupting.)* We've done that already. Now, how can we stop this 'marry Tartuffe' thing? Hmm… Okay, in this moment, your father is crazy for some reason. So, we have to delay things for a little times, until he is feeling more normal. You can say you are sick; or it is bad time to get married because of Brexit or something like this. You can keep coming up with excuses for months, then there is no wedding with Tartuffe, yes? But your father must not see you together. *(To WAQAAS.)* You, the Redditch Romeo, get out of here. We will get Mr. Khalil to help, and Amira. Go, don't worry is all going to be OK.

*WAQAAS looks into MARIAM's eyes as he holds her hand. DARINA
is ushering them to the door.*

WAQAAS: *(To MARIAM.)* I don't know what's going to happen
to us, but I do know one thing: I love you.

MARIAM: *(To WAQAAS.)* And I love you too! I would never
give myself to anyone but you!

WAQAAS: *(To MARIAM.)* And I would never let anyone take
you from me!

DARINA: Blah blah blah. *(To WAQAAS.)* Get out!

WAQAAS is about to go through the door.

WAQAAS: Bye.

MARIAM: Bye bye.

He goes but then pops back in again.

WAQAAS: I'm really sorry about before…

*DARINA pushes him out the door before he can finish, and slams the
door behind him, leaning against it in case he tries to get back in.*

MARIAM: Isn't he great?

DARINA: *(To audience.)* I preferred when they were arguing.

ACT III

SCENE 1

Living room. A garage/jungle tune is playing loudly on the bluetooth speaker. DAMEE is pacing around the living room, in a rage. He is smacking himself in the head with frustration whilst muttering to himself.

DAMEE: Inshallah. I can be with my baby for ever, my Zainab. My rani, my suraj. My jaan. Stay out of my way, your driving me insane, when you come into my name. Who does man think he is? Come in my yard. Disrespecting my family. Messing everything up… I'm going to sort him out, man. Opera man, I come phantom, Look at me I'm so handsome, smash his stupid little face in…come in my yard, man's not hard, spread him on my bread, like a tub full of lard…

DARINA comes in during this and watches him fondly. She nods at him and speaks to the audience.

DARINA: Ahhh. Poor Damee. He is lovely boy, but has, what we say in Bosnia, 'feathers for brain'.

DARINA unplugs the bluetooth speaker, cutting the music. DAMEE is punching the sofa. He notices DARINA.

DAMEE: Oh, hi Darina.

DARINA: Hello Damee.

DAMEE: Sorry about…

He stops punching the sofa and brushes it down.

DARINA: Is OK.

DAMEE: I'm just so fuc... *(Catches himself.)* I'm so piss...
   (Catches himself again.) I'm so cross about all this shit with
   Dad and shit.

DARINA: Yes.

DAMEE: You know what he's doing with Mariam now, innit?

DARINA: Yes.

DAMEE: He's only going make her marry that Tartuffe guy!

He slams his fist onto the table, knocking over an ornament.

Sorry.

DARINA picks up the ornament and replaces it.

It just makes me so vex. Tartuffe, man, he comes in
here and gives it large like he's king of the Muslims or
something. And Dad just eat it up like a pussy, like a pussy,
like a...pussy, pussy... Man's so fat. Give him nuff licks
with my baseball bat. It's a disgraceful act. Kussmeh, it's
war. W'allah'he I'm sure, he's up there, chillin' on my PS4.

He goes to hit something else.

DARINA: Wait!

She hands him a cushion from the sofa. He punches it as he rants...

DAMEE: I'm going to sort him out, man. Tell him I see him,
   innit. Tell him I ain't buying any of his holy man bullshit.
   Tell him...come on the scene, fakin' the deen, brer can't
   even fit in my skinny jeans...

DARINA: Wait!

*She takes the cushion, now nicely plumped, and hands him another
one. She throws a look to the audience – might as well make use
of him, eh?*

OK.

DAMEE continues punching the new cushion.

DAMEE: Tell him to get out of my dad's head and tell him
  he better leave my sister right alone or I'll fix him like
  he won't believe! Trust me. I got tricks up my sleeve, fix
  and believe, fix him and box, man don't stop, work like a
  stopcock, 'cause he loves to cockblock.

He gives the cushion a couple more thumps. DARINA takes it from him.

DARINA: OK. It's enough now. You need to calm down.

DAMEE: But…

DARINA: I know. But just because your father is say it, is not
  mean is going to happen.

DAMEE: Well I ain't taking any chances. Where is Tartuffe?

DARINA: OK, now, just hold on to your horse, hmmm?
  I have spoken with your stepmother about this.

DAMEE: Who?

DARINA: Amira.

DAMEE: Oh her.

DARINA: Amira will take care of it. She is going to speak to
  Tartuffy right now.

DAMEE: Amira's going to speak to him?

DARINA: Yes. He will listen to her. She will explain to him
  that this marriage with Mariam is bad idea.

DAMEE: How's she going to do that? She's not going to punch
  him.

DARINA: No. She use…other ways.

DAMEE: Like what?

DARINA: Your stepmother is very respected woman. She is very attractive woman. She is very intelligent woman. And Tartuffe is…man. *(Beat.)* You understand?

DAMEE: Yeah.

DARINA: So…

She gestures for him to leave.

DAMEE: So I need to be here too.

DARINA: No…

DAMEE: I got to make sure he don't get no funny ideas, you know what I mean?

DARINA: No, no, no. Leave it to us. It will all be OK…

She tries to usher him out of the door.

DAMEE: No, Darina, you don't understand. This is man thing. I got to sort it out with him, man to man. It's a question of honour. My family's honour. My sister's honour.

DARINA: Is funny. Men always talk about a woman's honour. They must defend their mother's honour. Their wife's honour. Their sister's honour. Why you not let women worry about their own honour, eh? I tell you why. Because it's not about woman's honour. It's about man's pride. Is about which man thinks he is in charge of this woman. But maybe, if men really cared about woman's honour, they would stop trying to control them. Stop trying to own them. Stop treating them like property and let woman decide for herself how she wants to live her life. That would be honourable thing to do.

DAMEE: Right. And you want me to tell Tartuffe that?

DARINA slaps her forehead, exasperated.

DARINA: Please Damee, be good boy. He is coming any
minute.

*She opens the door and checks. DAMEE folds his arms – he's not
budging. DARINA realises she need to change tack.*

OK, no, I see now you are right.

DAMEE: You do?

DARINA: Yes. You are man. This is important. You should be
here.

DAMEE: That is what I'm saying.

DARINA: But think how much better if Tartuffe is not knowing
you are here!

She steers him over to a large blanket box.

DAMEE: Eh?

DARINA: He will think he is on his own with Amira, but all
the time you will be here – out of sight.

DAMEE: So I'll be like…invisible?

DARINA: Yes. Like invisible. But hiding.

*She opens the blanket box and takes out a couple of blankets leaving
it empty. She gestures for DAMEE to get in. He does and she pushes
him down into the box.*

DAMEE: I'll be like the invisible man!

DARINA: You will be just like invisible man. Except also
completely silent like completely silent, invisible man.

DAMEE: Sick. *(She shuts the box and rolls her eyes.)*

SCENE 2

TARTUFFE enters. He wears a white collarless shirt with a long black 'cleric' style coat, a white skull cap and a long scarf. He is followed by his assistant, USMAN. USMAN is playing tablas and singing a haunting qawwali song in Urdu. TARTUFFE holds up a hand for USMAN to stop.

TARTUFFE: Ah, Usman. Your music feeds the soul,
when the cares of this world have taken their toll!

Thank you, my friend.

USMAN: *(Thick Brummie accent.)* No problem, anytime.

TARTUFFE speaks with a slight Arabic accent, which becomes more pronounced when he is making a religious point or speaking in verse. His accent will wander into Brummie in times of stress.

TARTUFFE: Usman, did you confirm with the foodbank that I'll be helping out there this afternoon?

USMAN: *(Brummie.)* They're expecting you at three.

TARTUFFE: Could you stay on top of my emails and Twitter feed until then? I want to spend the rest of the morning reciting from the Qu'ran.

DARINA: Shall I open windows? I don't think they heard you across the road.

TARTUFFE turns and pretends he's just noticed her.

TARTUFFE: Altariq 'iilaa albir mumtali jiddaan bialailti wa'at wallmunaeatafat kayf yumkinuni aistirjae almiah alty 'atuq 'iilyha?

A beat.

DARINA: No, I'm not understand any of that. Is it shopping list?

43

TARTUFFE: 'The road to the well is so full of twists and turns,
How can I retrieve the water forwhich I yearn?'

DARINA: Is it Elton John?

TARTUFFE: I'm just saying that we must work hard if we wish
to find Allah's truth.

DARINA: Some sort of 'job' might be good, then. Listen, I
want word with you.

*She approaches him. He suddenly flinches and turns away from
her, covering his eyes.*

TARTUFFE: Ah!

DARINA stops, confused.

Cover yourself, woman!

USMAN: Cover yourself!

He takes the scarf from round his shoulders and waves it at her.

TARTUFFE: Take this, take it!

USMAN: Take it!

TARTUFFE: And cover your immodesty, lest it should offend
Allah. And in case it corrupts my mind with sinful thoughts!

USMAN: Don't corrupt his mind!

*DARINA shakes her head, but takes the scarf and drapes it across
her chest. TARTUFFE peeks through his fingers.*

TARTUFFE: No, no. Your hair. Cover your hair.

USMAN: Hair!

She shrugs and wraps the scarf around her head.

DARINA: *(To audience.)* I don't know why he is worried about
seeing my hair. I could see whole of his naked body and it

44

not do nothing for me. *(She looks him up and down.)* In fact, would put me right off.

TARTUFFE: This is a Muslim household, which Allah has chosen to protect. So all of us within it, must show Him our respect.

DARINA: By covering hair?

TARTUFFE: Yes. In Islam women must cover their hair to show their reverence to Allah.

DARINA: Why?

TARTUFFE exchanges a look with USMAN – oh dear.

TARTUFFE: *(As to an idiot.)* What you have to understand, my dear, is that we have a holy book called the Qu'ran. It is the direct word of Allah, and, as such, is the source of all laws for the practice of true Islam.

DARINA: You are talking about chapter twenty-four verse thirty-one.

He looks to USMAN for help. USMAN shrugs then has an idea, takes out the iPhone and starts googling it.

(Interrupting.) Don't bother googling it – I've checked. It says '…and they should place their khumur over their bosoms.' Bosoms. Nothing about 'hair' or 'head'.

TARTUFFE: Well 'khumur'…

DARINA: You can argue about the translation of 'khumur'. But I choose this way. And that is between me and Allah.

TARTUFFE: Now look…

DARINA: And if it bothers you so much, maybe you should think about verse thirty.

TARTUFFE has no idea. He nods to USMAN to google again.

45

DARINA: 'The men should cast down their glances.' So stop looking!

TARTUFFE: I'm not going to stand here and be lectured on Islam by a Polish cleaner!

DARINA: Bosniak.

TARTUFFE: Hmm?

DARINA: Not Polish. I am Bosniak. A Bosnian Muslim. From Bosnia.

A beat.

TARTUFFE: Well, I don't know what kind of corrupt, decadent, westernised version of the faith you get up to in 'Bosnia', but what I'm talking about is the real Qu'ran, in Arabic, that proper Muslims use.

DARINA: 'Proper' Muslims?

TARTUFFE: Brown ones.

DARINA: *(Cursing him.)* Seronja magarac…

TARTUFFE covers his ears.

TARTUFFE: *(To USMAN.)* As Allah has closed their ears to the truth, so we must close our own when they become… uncouth.

DARINA: Don't worry, I go now. But the mistress want me to tell you she is coming to have talk.

TARTUFFE: Amira wants to talk to me?

DARINA: Yes.

TARTUFFE: Well, I'll wait for her, of course!

DARINA: Of course. *(To audience.)* Look at him. Is like little boy outside candy shop. As we say in Bosnia, he is 'fancy the panties off her'.

TARTUFFE is checking himself out in the mirror.

TARTUFFE: Did she say how long she'd be?

DARINA is at the door. She looks, opens it and checks.

DARINA: She's here now.

DARINA takes the scarf off and throws it to TARTUFFE. He catches it and quickly arranges it around his shoulders as AMIRA enters.

SCENE 3

AMIRA: Hi!

TARTUFFE: Asalaam aleikum!

AMIRA: Oh, yes, Waleikum Salaam.

TARTUFFE waves at USMAN to go. He doesn't get it and looks puzzled. TARTUFFE continues to shoo him whilst gushing at AMIRA.

TARTUFFE: May Allah continue to bestow his countless blessings upon you.

AMIRA: Thank you.

More shooing. USMAN still not getting it.

TARTUFFE: And may he protect you and watch over you and grant you peace and happiness and, you know, a really, really long life.

AMIRA: How nice.

TARTUFFE waves at USMAN again. USMAN waves back.

TARTUFFE: And may you always… *(Shouts at USMAN.)* Go away!

USMAN: Oh!

The penny drops for USMAN. He leaves.

AMIRA: I beg your pardon?

TARTUFFE: Not you! Sorry, it was… I was…doesn't matter.

An awkward beat.

So…

AMIRA: Would you like to sit down?

TARTUFFE: That would be fantastic.

TARTUFFE checks his breath by cupping his hands over his mouth, maybe sprays himself surreptitiously with some aftershave. They sit. A beat.

How are you? Are you feeling better? I heard you had a headache.

AMIRA: I'm much better thank you.

TARTUFFE affects a poetic stance and confidently begins speaking in couplets. He moves around her as he does so.

TARTUFFE: I'm so pleased to hear it because, you see
I have been praying for you constantly.

AMIRA: Oh. Er, thanks…?

TARTUFFE: About your health you should take heed,
'Tis more important than my own indeed.

AMIRA: Right. Is this going to be…

TARTUFFE: I would as soon give of my good health to you,
As a gift, and you'd see my concern is true.

AMIRA: OK.

TARTUFFE: But you assure me that you are quite well?

AMIRA: I do…

TARTUFFE: Then come, let us sit a spell…

He guides her to sit.

AMIRA: I had no idea you were such a…

TARTUFFE: … Poet? An artist? A lover of verse?

AMIRA: If you like.
I was going to say something much worse.

TARTUFFE: You tease me then,
but I know it's meant as good-hearted.

AMIRA: Well give me a chance.
I've only just started.

TARTUFFE: You know I feel there's something between us,
it's definitely there.

AMIRA: The chair?

TARTUFFE: A connection.

AMIRA: Such things are quite rare.

TARTUFFE: We cannot ignore it, it would be a crime.
Don't you feel something different?

She shakes her head.

AMIRA: Just the talking in rhyme.

TARTUFFE: Well that must tell you something.

AMIRA: It's novel, I'll grant.

TARTUFFE: More than that surely.
Deny it.

AMIRA is about to reply. TARTUFFE jumps in.

You can't! As characters in a play we are become,
Like Shakespeare. Or that French one.
You must concede, at the very least, it shows,
A mutual understanding?

AMIRA: ... I don't think so, no.
It's over it's finished, the moment was fleeting...

TARTUFFE: I'm just getting started.

AMIRA: ...and you're over-heating.

TARTUFFE hesitates for a moment.

TARTUFFE: As you wish.

AMIRA indicates for him to sit down next to her. To the side, DAMEE raises the lid of the blanket box and peeks out.

AMIRA: Now, I wanted to speak with you about a rather... delicate matter.

TARTUFFE: Oh good.

AMIRA: What?

TARTUFFE: I mean, I've been wanting to talk with you too. About your delicate matters. In a spiritual sense.

AMIRA: I thought it best to do it in private.

TARTUFFE: Absolutely.

He moves closer to her.

AMIRA: Away from prying eyes and ears.

There is a bang as DAMEE ducks back down and the lid of the blanket box shuts. They both look round, see nothing, and shrug.

So...

TARTUFFE: So...?

AMIRA: I've heard Imran thinks that you would be a good match for Mariam.

TARTUFFE: *(Not what he was hoping for.)* Oh.

AMIRA: Is it true?

TARTUFFE: Er, yes, I think he might have mentioned something about it.

AMIRA: And?

TARTUFFE: And…?

AMIRA: You're not considering it?

TARTUFFE: Imran has become a very close friend. I like to think that I have helped him on his spiritual journey and I am honoured that he would want to have me as his son-in-law.

AMIRA: Yes but…

TARTUFFE: But?

AMIRA: Well, I mean, the fact is, you and me, we're grown-ups. Adults. And Mariam, she's really still just a girl. Do you know what I mean?

TARTUFFE: Oh absolutely. She's just a kid. Whereas, as you say, I'm a man. And you're very much…a woman.

He leans in even closer to her.

AMIRA: So you agree, it's a bad idea?

TARTUFFE: What is?

AMIRA: You and Mariam.

TARTUFFE: To be honest, I'm really not thinking about that right now.

AMIRA: Because your mind is set on higher things?

TARTUFFE: Not exactly.

He glances at AMIRA's chest. AMIRA misses this.

AMIRA: Oh. I'm so sorry!

TARTUFFE: What? What is it?

AMIRA: Please, I hope I haven't offended you.

TARTUFFE: Why? What have you done?

AMIRA: My hair. My head's uncovered.

TARTUFFE: And?

AMIRA: I should have worn hijab.

TARTUFFE: There's no need.

AMIRA: But I know how strongly you feel about these things.

TARTUFFE: Ah, well, interestingly, what a lot of people don't realise is that there is no specific reference in the Qu'ran to a woman wearing hijab.

AMIRA: Really?

TARTUFFE: This is a common misunderstanding. The texts talk about modesty of dress, covering certain areas, but there is no requirement to cover hair.

AMIRA looks down at what she's wearing.

AMIRA: I'll go and get changed…

TARTUFFE: No! Honestly it's fine. You look boobiful. Beautiful. And, you know, this is your home. I think you can be a bit more relaxed here. I mean, I'm not some sort of fanatic! I can be very laid back, in the right circumstances.

AMIRA: But you're not my husband. Or my son. Or my brother. Or my husband's father. Or…

TARTUFFE: No, no, I know. But I feel that we are very close. I'm almost like family, in a way. You could think of me like that.

AMIRA: Like my son?

TARTUFFE: No!

AMIRA: Brother then.

TARTUFFE: Not your brother.

AMIRA: A cousin?

TARTUFFE: Do you like your cousins?

AMIRA: Not much.

TARTUFFE: Then not a cousin either.

AMIRA: I'll go and change…

She gets up and heads for the door. He jumps up and grabs her hand.

TARTUFFE: Please, wait! Don't go!

AMIRA stops and stares at his hand holding hers. He drops her hand immediately.

Sorry. It's just…please…

He beckons for her to sit back down. She does so, reluctantly. He sits down next to her, then inches closer.

Thank you. Honestly, the way you're dressed is fine. More than fine! You look amazing. *(Feeling her salwaar.)* This is lovely material. Is it polycotton?

AMIRA: Hardly.

TARTUFFE: It's a beautiful pattern. Amazing what they can do nowadays. So complex, so delicate, *(voice trembling slightly)* so *thin...*

AMIRA: Mr. Arsuf, I really don't think...

TARTUFFE: Oh, call me Tartuffe, please. We are at least friends, aren't we?

AMIRA: I suppose, but...

TARTUFFE: Perhaps, if I could just tell you how I feel...

AMIRA: I'm not sure that's a...

TARTUFFE: You are the most beautiful woman I have ever seen! All other women are as nothing beside you. Your beauty is so great it would put heaven itself and all the angels to shame. I am in awe of your physical perfection. Your eyes are like emeralds from Kashmir, your lips like the reddest rubies from Persia, your hair, long and lustrous and is jet black but shimmers and shines like the desert sky!

TARTUFFE pauses, breathless. AMIRA decides there are worse things to listen to.

AMIRA: Go on.

TARTUFFE: I could gaze at you for eternity and still find new things to marvel at. The curve of your neck as it slides into your shoulder...the curve of your shoulder as it turns into your arm...the curve of your...

AMIRA: I really don't think this is appropriate...

TARTUFFE: It's OK. There's nothing to be ashamed of. The Qu'ran wants us to celebrate beauty. It talks about 'zeena', the special kind of beauty that is given only to women. That's the Pakistani Qu'ran, too, so it must be right.

AMIRA: But I'm married, and you're a scholar and a servant of Allah.

TARTUFFE: *(Raising his voice.)* But I'm only human! Made of flesh and blood.

AMIRA: Shhh! Keep your voice down.

TARTUFFE: This is actually your fault you know!

AMIRA: My fault?

TARTUFFE: If you weren't so attractive, I wouldn't be tempted!

AMIRA: I'm sorry. It must be difficult for you.

TARTUFFE: *(Shaking his head.)* It's a burden all righteous men have to bear. But look, it's okay. If you and I do… *(He nods and raises his eyebrows.)* You know… I wouldn't tell anyone. I know a lot of guys would go bragging about it to all their mates, posting pictures on Facebook and all that. But you have my solemn word, I won't mention it to a soul. Not even on Twitter.

AMIRA: What a gentleman.

TARTUFFE suddenly reaches out and puts his hand over her breast. He leaves it there for a few seconds. They both look at it. Then he takes it away. A beat.

TARTUFFE: Forgive me. I don't know what… Your beauty overwhelmed me! I couldn't help myself!

AMIRA stares at him. Did you really just do that?

I misread the signals. We were talking, you did the rhyming… I thought…

AMIRA: You thought that meant 'feel free to grab my breast'?

TARTUFFE: Look, this was a simple misunderstanding. I've apologised, you've accepted. No harm done. We should keep it between ourselves. There's no need to tell anyone else.

AMIRA: Like…my husband.

TARTUFFE: Exactly. He mustn't know. I mean it would only upset him.

AMIRA: Do you think? To hear that the holy man of Allah he brought into his home was trying to seduce his wife? That the pious follower of Islam was actually a gropey little letch?

TARTUFFE: Then don't tell him!

A long beat, while AMIRA pretends to decide what to do and TARTUFFE squirms.

AMIRA: You know what, I'm going to give you the benefit of the doubt. I won't say anything to Imran…

TARTUFFE: *(To the heavens, relieved.)* Thank you!

AMIRA: On one condition. That you tell him that you aren't interested in Mariam, and that he should let her marriage to Waqaas go ahead without…

TARTUFFE is about to agree. DAMEE leaps up from out of the blanket box.

SCENE 4

DAMEE: Stop!

TARTUFFE: *(Brummie.)* Bloody hell!

TARTUFFE tries to leap away, and falls off his chair.

DAMEE: Get away from her!

TARTUFFE stands up and backs away.

TARTUFFE: *(Brummie.)* I wasn't doing anything!

AMIRA: Damee, whats going on?

DAMEE: It's alright, I've got this. *(To TARTUFFE.)* How dare you touch up my stepmother!

TARTUFFE composes himself.

TARTUFFE: *(Arabic again.)* I was just feeling her salwaar kameez.

DAMEE: I know what you were feeling!

AMIRA: Really it's fine. It's no big deal.

DAMEE: I know what I saw.

AMIRA: Nothing happened, it's all under control. And Tartuffe, Mr. Arsuf, is very sorry, aren't you?

TARTUFFE nods vigorously.

And I've told him it won't go any further, so let's just leave it at that, shall we?

DAMEE: No way, blud. Someone needs to defend your honour. Our honour. He's been taking the piss out of us for too long, and I'm going to put an end to it right now!

AMIRA: Damee, please, calm down...

TARTUFFE: Yes, calm down, Damee...

DAMEE turns on him, TARTUFFE flinches.

DAMEE: Shut it, you twat.

TARTUFFE: OK.

AMIRA: Can we talk about this later?

DAMEE: No. No more talking. There's been enough talking. Now it's time for doing.

AMIRA: What are you going to do?

DAMEE: I'm going to tell Dad! *(Realises.)* Which...is also talking but that's not the same thing as the talking...you get me!

IMRAN enters.

IMRAN: Asalaam Aleikum!

TARTUFFE/AMIRA: Waleikum Salaam.

DAMEE: Dad! You won't believe…

IMRAN: Damee! I said 'Asalaam Aleikum'.

DAMEE: What? Oh, right, yeah, Waleikum Salaam. But, listen, you're not going to believe what…

IMRAN: *(To TARTUFFE.)* You see, Tartuffeji, this is what's wrong with our young people these days. He doesn't even return my Salaam.

DAMEE: Dad! Please!

IMRAN: Dad, he says! Not Sir. Not Abbujaan. Dad.

IMRAN shakes his head, disappointed.

DAMEE: OK, Dad, Sir, Abbu, whatever. You think I'm bad, but I've just caught Amira –

IMRAN: Ammi-jaan!

DAMEE: Listen I've just caught this lying, two-faced, scumbag trying to get it on with Ammi-jaan!

IMRAN: What?!

AMIRA shakes her head.

DAMEE: Yeah. You bring him into your house, treat him like he's the prophet Mohammed himself…

TARTUFFE/IMRAN: Peace be upon him.

DAMEE: Yeah, well, this is how he repays you. By copping off with your wife, in your own living room. She didn't want to tell you, probably to spare your feelings or some shit like that. But we're men, and this is a question of honour.

AMIRA: *(To IMRAN.)* I wasn't going to tell you because there's nothing to tell. *(To DAMEE.)* And as far as my honour's concerned, I'm quite capable of looking after it myself. It was all in hand…

DAMEE: Too bloody right it was!

AMIRA: And, just for once, you should have listened to me and kept well out of it!

She leaves. IMRAN goes to follow her then stops. A beat. IMRAN looks from DAMEE to TARTUFFE.

IMRAN: Amira, Amira, I can't believe this.

DAMEE: I know!

IMRAN: To walk into your own living room and hear such things…

TARTUFFE: Please my brother. Before you say anything, let me say this. There can be no doubt that I am a guilty man. I am a sinner. I have sinned in the past, and I have sinned today. I'll probably sin again in the future. I have committed all manner of sins, great and small, both Dhunub and Khati'ah. So listen to your son. Hear what he says, and know that he is right… I'm not worthy of your kindness. I'm not worthy of your hospitality or your trust. You should turn me out onto the street where you found me, for it's no more than I deserve.

IMRAN stares at TARTUFFE.

IMRAN: You selfish, foul, spiteful, wretch.

DAMEE: Yeah.

Then DAMEE realises IMRAN has turned and is addressing him.

59

Wait, what?

IMRAN: You disgust me.

DAMEE: Me!

IMRAN: How dare you accuse this man, this angel, of such a terrible thing?

DAMEE: No way. You're not still buying into all his holy moly bullshit…?

IMRAN: Enough! Enough of your filth!

TARTUFFE: No, let him speak! He's right. Why should you think good of me and ill of him? He is your son, your own flesh and blood. And who am I? Just some bloke you met at the mosque. What do you really know about me? Sure, I dress humbly, and respectfully, like a true Muslim. But so what? Yes I can recite from the Qu'ran. I can recite the hadith. But what does that prove? Does that make me the better man? No. Who cares how many times I go to the mosque? How often I pray. Who cares if the whole community thinks I'm some kind of spiritual leader? Only Allah the great and merciful can truly know and judge me. *(To DAMEE.)* So go ahead. Call me a liar. Call me a cheat. Call me what you like. It's no more than I deserve.

TARTUFFE falls to his knees, arms outspread. IMRAN gasps.

IMRAN: Oh! No, please, Tartuffeji… *(To DAMEE.)* Well?

DAMEE: You're not serious? Man's a chupid wasterman.

IMRAN: Be quiet! I won't hear any more. *(To TARTUFFE.)* Please, brother, sit down, I beg you. *(To DAMEE.)* You see what you've done? Happy now?

DAMEE: But…

IMRAN: Chup!

DAMEE: Dad!

IMRAN: Chupp! I should give you one thappad...!

He raises his hand to DAMEE.

TARTUFFE: Hold, brother! Strike me instead of him. He doesn't know any better, he's just a boy.

IMRAN: He's an ungrateful little shit...

TARTUFFE: But he's *your* ungrateful little shit. Forgive him.

IMRAN throws himself to his knees and embraces TARTUFFE.

IMRAN: Oh, we don't deserve you. *(To DAMEE.)* You see? You see what kind of man he is?

DAMEE: Yeah. I can. Why can't you?

IMRAN: I know what this is really all about. You've never liked him. None of you. From the moment I brought him home, I sensed it. And I know why as well. Because he's shown us how far from the righteous path we've strayed. He sees you all with your fashion, and your devices and your debit cards and your nightclubs and he doesn't see true Muslims. You're all in love with your hashtag lifestyles and you're afraid of him because he knows how meaningless that all is. This man has given me more then any of you ever have. And that's why I want him to become a part of our family.

DAMEE: You're not really going to make Mariam marry this prick, are you? She hates him.

IMRAN: Not true! Not true. Mariam is a good girl and she knows that I only have her best interests at heart. *(To TARTUFFE.)* This marriage will give me a son to be proud of. The son I've always wanted.

DAMEE: What? Dad! I'm your son!

61

IMRAN gets up and confronts DAMEE.

IMRAN: Are you? Look at you. They way you dress. The way you talk. We're Muslim, Damee. Pakistani Muslim. But you, you're more like some foreign English delinquent.

DAMEE: I was born here!

TARTUFFE: I think what your father means is that it is our spiritual selves which should define us. It is our faith which gives us our true identities, as Pakistani Muslims.

DAMEE: You're from Small Heath!

IMRAN: He is a man of Allah and a true Muslim.

DAMEE: Oh what, so maybe I should piss off to Syria and start shooting at women and kids. Is that what true Muslims do?

TARTUFFE: I will never condemn a man, it's true, for acting as his faith tells him to.

DAMEE: Are you freestyling at me, bro?
Cos if you wanna go, toe to toe
I'll put you in the ground below.

TARTUFFE: But in the ground, like a seed I'm sown,
From an acorn to an oak tree I've grown.

DAMEE: Please – leave the raps alone, you're lame,
This is my house and this is my game…

TARTUFFE: It really isn't me who's forgotten his place,
Look at your father you're a damn disgrace!

DAMEE: I'm not a disgrace, if I'm a disgrace,
you're a sham to your race,
with your holier than thou act up in this place.
You're about to get waste,
'cause I'm about to pull trigger and blow up your…

62

Opera man, I come phantom
Look at me I'm so handsome
You be baby like tantrum
Steal my dad just like ransom
Ain't no way you're succeeding
I'mma cut his face 'til he's bleeding
Blood sprinkle like seasoning
Real talk, I'm not preaching
This right here is a certainty
I'm a stone cold killer, yeah third degree
I'mma merk man so hungrily
Spread you on my bread like Dairylea. Cheese!

TARTUFFE: I'm a, I'm a, I'm a Twitter, blue tick
A million hits a day
And you don't have shit to say
So sit and hit PayPal to buy you one follow bot
Lost in the rot
Of the western lies you swallow
Is a hollow entity
You borrow a black man's identity
While I'm Pakistan relentlessly
And I preach it with empathy
Endlessy
I teach about the heavenly
Ma' Shallah
Your weakness is jealously
Inshallah
You won't ever be ahead of me
Even the head of the house
Treats me like the son you'll never be
Alhamdullilah
Your dead mother
Would have smothered you
At birth
Rather than inflict your curse

On the earth
For what are you worth
Astagfirullah
You don't even pray
Astagfirullah
You sin every day
Astagfirullah
Your father, your sister, your PS4
Even your Dadimaa, I'm taking them all.

IMRAN: *(To TARTUFFE.)* I blame myself for this. I've been too soft with them. Let them lose their way. I'll send him back to Pakistan. *(To DAMEE.)* You can stay with your uncle in Rawalpindi. He'll put you back on the straight and narrow. You can leave tomorrow.

DAMEE: No bloody way. I've got tickets for Glastonbury.

IMRAN: We are Pakistani Muslims, Damee. You will respect your father and do as I say.

DAMEE: What's being Pakistani got to do with it anyway? Even the prophet Mohammed...

IMRAN/TARTUFFE: Peace be upon him.

DAMEE: ...wasn't bloody Pakistani.

IMRAN freezes.

IMRAN: How dare you! That's the second time you have dishonoured the name of the Prophet.

IMRAN/TARTUFFE: Peace be upon him.

IMRAN: *(To TARTUFFE.)* I apologise for my son. He shames me.

TARTUFFE: There's no need. You are a good man. A good father. You have done your best, bringing them up without a mother...

64

IMRAN: *(To DAMEE.)* At least she's not here to see what you've become.

DAMEE is shocked.

DAMEE: What...

IMRAN: She would never allow you to act in this way. You are dishonouring her memory.

DAMEE: Me! What are you doing? Honouring her? Respecting her? Showing how much she meant to you by hooking up with some dolly bird from work. Bringing her into my mum's family, my mum's house! My mum's bed...

IMRAN is in DAMEE's face, on the cusp of striking him, but stops himself. He steps back and speaks with a chilling calm.

IMRAN: Get out. Get out of my house.

DAMEE doesn't move. Now IMRAN shouts.

Get out! I want nothing more to do with you. You're not my son. You are not part of this family any more. Go!

DAMEE stares at IMRAN, incredulous. IMRAN stares back, pointing at the door. TARTUFFE gets up from his knees and stands behind IMRAN. Eventually DAMEE turns and stomps out, slamming the door.

And never come back!

(To TARTUFFE.) I'm so sorry...

SCENE 6

TARTUFFE: Please, I'm sure he didn't mean it.

IMRAN: I'm afraid he's lost. There's no way back.

TARTUFFE: 'Despair not of the mercy of Allah, for Allah forgives all sins. For he is oft forgiving.'

IMRAN: You are too good for us.

TARTUFFE: Not at all. Although I must say some of the things he was saying were really quite hurtful.

IMRAN: The bastard!

TARTUFFE: Really, it's fine. But look, I can see that my presence here is only going to cause more trouble. Perhaps it's best if I went...

IMRAN: What! No!

TARTUFFE: They don't like me. You said it yourself.

IMRAN: That's just Damee. Mariam likes you. Amira likes you.

TARTUFFE: Your cleaner doesn't like me.

IMRAN: No. But she doesn't like anyone.

TARTUFFE: Why don't you fire her?

IMRAN: Do you know how hard it is to get a good cleaner? Please, there's no need for you to leave.

TARTUFFE: Maybe not now. But you know how people talk. Community gossip. I wouldn't want to embarrass you.

IMRAN: Don't be silly. I never listen to all that rubbish anyway.

TARTUFFE: But if it keeps on and on. The whispers in the shop. People sniggering at the mosque.

IMRAN: Let them snigger.

TARTUFFE: Who knows, even Amira might decide she's had enough of me around one day. She could say anything.

IMRAN: Don't be ridiculous.

TARTUFFE: I'll go, and then you never need worry...

IMRAN: No, please. I'm begging you. We need you. I need you.

A beat. TARTUFFE savours the moment.

TARTUFFE: Very well. I'll stay.

IMRAN breathes a sigh of relief.

But to avoid any scandal, maybe it's best if I steer clear of Amira from now on.

IMRAN: Nonsense. I want you to spend as much time as possible with her. You need to show her that she's not walking the true path of Islam. Help her to find the right way to live. Talk to her. Teach her. Do to her what you have done with me.

TARTUFFE: I might do it slightly differently with her.

IMRAN: Whatever you think. You're the expert.

TARTUFFE: You're too kind.

IMRAN: And Brother, I've been thinking. Before you came along I was so caught up in the trappings of decadent western capitalism, I was blind to my faith. It does that, the house, the business, the money, the Norwegian spruce decking. It consumes you.

TARTUFFE: It is not the consumer society but the consuming society!

IMRAN: Exactly. And my wife, my daughter, they're still caught up in all of that.

TARTUFFE: It is hard to see past such shiny baubles.

IMRAN: So I was wondering if you would do me a huge favour. I mean, I know I have no right to ask, you've done so much already...

TARTUFFE: Please, my brother, it is not only my duty but my pleasure to help others.

IMRAN: I want to sign everything over to you. The house, the business, the decking, all of it. Leave us free to walk in the light of Allah. Please take from us this burden.

A beat as TARTUFFE digests this.

TARTUFFE: Go on then.

ACT IV

SCENE 1

Lights on, but the stage is empty. We hear a vacuum cleaner in the stalls. DARINA comes in from the back of the stalls with her hoover, cleaning down the aisles and under the seats.

DARINA: Excuse please. Move feets. You alright there, having good time? You with family? No? Someone else's family? I won't say anything. You got choc ice, eh? Last of big spenders. Be careful when you eat. No drips on chair. And take wrapper with you! I got enough to do without wiping up your sticky mess.

She has reached the stage.

So. Let me see… *(To self – mentally ticking off jobs.)* Out there, done, kitchen, done, under the stairs loo, done… *(To audience.)* Sorry I have to remember what I do on Thursday. *(To 'stupid' audience member.)* Today is Thursday. Before was Monday. I come Monday and Thursday. I know! Twice a week. But you seen this family. They need lot of help. Don't worry, you haven't missed anything. Imran kicked out Damee, you saw that bit didn't you? Okay so then…family was very upset…there was more shouting and crying, and then Imran went away on business trip. Typical man – make big mess then leave everybody else to clean up afterwards.

TARTUFFE enters the living room, followed by KHALIL. TARTUFFE is on his phone, checking his Twitter feed.

She leaves. KHALIL waits until she's gone, smiling politely at her as she goes out.

KHALIL: I'm just saying that given the family situation…

TARTUFFE: Mmm…

KHALIL: …the duty of care inherent in your influential position…

TARTUFFE: Mmm…

KAHLIL: *(Sees DARINA.)* Oh, sorry.

DARINA: Is OK. I'm finish.

KHALIL: Alright as I was saying, the duty of care inherent in your influential position, which you can't fail to acknowledge having stressed that influence on many occasions…

TARTUFFE: Is there a main clause on the way anytime soon, because I've got a busy day ahead…

KHALIL: …can't you just forget the whole thing and move on? I mean, let's assume that Damee is out of order, and that he's accused you of something that didn't happen; maybe he feels in some way that he's been *disrespected* by you – I know that can be an issue within Black Asian and minority ethnic 'street' culture… Now, if you'll give me a moment to pursue this scenario, where Damee has trespassed against you, if you like, shouldn't you, as a man of Allah, forgive him? For doesn't the Qur'an tell us that Allah himself is full of forgiveness? 'If your sins were to reach the clouds of the sky and then you were to seek my forgiveness, I would forgive you.'

TARTUFFE: I think you might be using the wrong translation.

KHALIL: *(Smug.)* Pretty sure I'm using the right one!

TARTUFFE: You mean the *white* one.

KHALIL: You can't allow a son to be kicked out of his father's house over a little tiff like this. People will gossip about it. Your reputation will suffer!

TARTUFFE: Now look Colin...do you mind if I call you Colin.

He puts his arm round KHALIL's shoulder. KHALIL looks at TARTUFFE's arm.

KHALIL: My name is Khalil.

TARTUFFE: Not your real name.

KHALIL: It is my Muslim name. I would have thought you of all people could respect that.

TARTUFFE: Of course. The thing is Colin, I'd love to help them out, I really would. As far as I'm concerned it's all water under the bridge – I've got no beef with Damee at all. He's a good lad, and there's nothing I want more than to forgive him his little outburst and for us all go back to being friends again...

KHALIL is about to thank him for his forbearance.

KHALIL: Well, that would be wonderful...

TARTUFFE: ...but Allah doesn't want me to.

KHALIL: Right.

TARTUFFE: You see, if Damee comes back home, I'd have to leave, wouldn't I.

KHALIL: Would you?

TARTUFFE: *(Convoluted explanation.)* Yes, because, look – if I was to let him come back after all the terrible but imaginary things he's accused me of doing, people would say I was actually admitting that what he'd said about me was true, and that in fact those terrible imaginary things weren't actually imaginary at all but actually terrible and I was only letting him come back in order to keep him quiet about those actually terrible non-imaginary things that I did, in fact, actually do. Do you see?

KHALIL: Not really.

TARTUFFE: Look, Colin, forgiveness is all very well. But piety is more important. And I cannot have people doubting my piety even if their doubts are based upon falsehood.

KHALIL: But that doesn't make any sense. Surely Allah is the only one who can judge your piety. If you think about it rationally...

TARTUFFE: I don't need to be rational. I need to follow the word of Allah. Islam is not about rationality, Colin. Logic and science, these are the tools of the godless. You modernists like to talk about rationality, but I'm a traditional Muslim. A 'real' Muslim. We've been doing things this way for 1400 years. There's no reason to change now.

KHALIL: Actually, if I could just arrest your flow that's not strictly true. Islamic scholars were at the forefront of scientific progress hundreds of years before the west even got started.

TARTUFFE: Were they really?

KHALIL: The Umayyad and er...

TARTUFFE: Abbasid?

KHALIL: ...Abbasid caliphates promoted the sciences as early as the eighth century.

TARTUFFE: I'm glad you're here to whitemansplain our own history to us.

KHALIL: So of course you'll be aware of Al- Battani, whose cosmological tables were used by Copernicus, and of Al- Khwarizmi's development of algebra, and of the huge leaps in medical understanding made by Ibn-Sina.

TARTUFFE: Spend a lot of time on Wikipedia, do you?

KHALIL: I'm just making the point that far from science and learning and the quest for knowledge being a western invention, it was actually thanks to Islamic scholars that the knowledge accrued by the ancient civilisations...

TARTUFFE: Colin, Colin, Colin. That was the old days. Things are different now.

KHALIL: How did we get to a point where the most tolerant and academically inquisitive religion in the world ended up being hijacked by people like you?

TARTUFFE: That's progress for you!

KHALIL: Just let the boy come back home.

TARTUFFE: Sorry, can't do it.

KHALIL: And will it make Allah happy if you take possession of a house that doesn't belong to you?

Beat.

TARTUFFE: Colin, I am not doing any of this for myself. Worldly possessions have no meaning for me. In fact, the only reason I'm accepting this...small token of Imran's esteem, is because I worry what will happen to it if it falls into someone else's hands.

Other people might not use it to do the work of Allah and help the poor.

KHALIL: But didn't Imam al Baqir...

TARTUFFE: Shia!

KHALIL: ...the sage, the great teacher, the first Imam...

TARTUFFE: Shia Imam!

KHALIL: ...descended from both grandsons of the prophet...

KHALIL/USMAN: Peace be upon him.

KHALIL: ...say that...

TARTUFFE: Sorry, can I just stop you there?

KHALIL: Yes?

TARTUFFE taps his watch.

TARTUFFE: Prayer time!

KHALIL: What?

TARTUFFE: Got to go. Really interesting to talk to you, though! *(He shakes KHALIL's hand.)*

KHALIL: Yes, we'll continue this discussion...

TARTUFFE leaves.

...later.

SCENE 2

AMIRA, DARINA and MARIAM enter.

AMIRA: Did you talk to Tartuffe about Damee?

KHALIL: Yes, I did.

AMIRA: And?

KHALIL: He hasn't changed his mind.

AMIRA: What about Imran, did you call him?

KHALIL: Yes I did.

DARINA: And?

KHALIL: He hasn't changed his mind either.

MARIAM has been waiting to say her bit.

MARIAM: What about the wedding?

KHALIL: The wedding?

DARINA: Marrying her off to this arse Tartuffe.

KHALIL: I think he prefers 'Holy Man'?

DARINA: Fine, this asshole-y man, Tartuffe?

A beat.

KHALIL: We didn't get on to that.

SCENE 3

IMRAN enters.

IMRAN: Asalaam Aleikum.

ALL: Waleikum Salaam.

IMRAN: What a journey! You would not believe the traffic on
the M40...

He takes an invitation out of his pocket.

IMRAN: So, Mariam, beti, I've had the invites to your
wedding printed up. What do you think? The lettering's a
bit fancy but we can change that...

MARIAM: No...

IMRAN: The sooner we get this done the better. *(He's actually
going through with it.)*

MARIAM: Dad, you can't organise a wedding.

IMRAN: Um, yes, I can. I have a business hiring out wedding
venues? It's pretty easy.

IMRAN delves in his briefcase.

MARIAM: *(To DARINA and AMIRA.)* I thought you had a plan?

MARIAM looks at AMIRA. AMIRA doesn't respond. IMRAN retrieves some paperwork from his briefcase.

IMRAN: Here – we've drawn up the nikaah contract. You just need to sign it. And then in the eyes of Allah you will be Mrs. Tartuffe Arsuf.

MARIAM: Now?

IMRAN: Yes, now! This family needs strong guidance. I've already lost Damee because of my weakness, I don't want to lose you too.

He touches her face, smiling fondly. She gets down on her knees, takes his hand.

MARIAM: *(Realising she's dealing with a crazy man, trying to appeal to his newfound religious zeal.)* Papaji, if you won't listen to me, then listen to Allah! Can you hear him? He's telling you not to do this! He can see I'm desperate, can't he? He sees everything, right? He knows if you make me marry someone else, someone I don't even like…he knows I can't do that. He knows I'd rather kill myself!

IMRAN: *(Struggling with his conscience.)* Beti, this is for your own good. It's definitely the right thing to do. Definitely.

MARIAM: Give him everything else. Give him the house, the business, give him all of it. But don't give him me.

A beat. AMIRA watches from the other side of the room, growing angrier by the minute. IMRAN has pause for a moment then shakes off the doubt.

IMRAN: *(To KHALIL.)* Women! Everything's always such a drama, eh? *(He lifts her up gently by the hand.)* Come on, beti. The harder this is for you, the better it's going to be for your relationship with Allah.

MARIAM: Please, Dad, this is insane!

IMRAN: *(Gently.)* You need to learn the discipline, you see? To be pious. Piety is the discipline of denying yourself what *you* want, and accepting what *Allah* wants.

DARINA: Tell me Mister, why it is always women who must deny themselves what they want?

IMRAN: You keep out if it. This doesn't concern you. You're just the cleaner.

DARINA: And you're full of shit!

IMRAN: How dare you use such profanity in front of my daughter!

DARINA: You are right, I'm sorry. I am not showing enough respect to her, like you do. Please carry on forcing her to have sex with man she hates.

KHALIL: If I could just offer a word of advice at this point...

IMRAN/DARINA: No!

KHALIL: OK.

IMRAM: Sign it.

AMIRA decides it's time to act.

AMIRA: You're actually doing this, are you?

IMRAN: What's that?

AMIRA: You're seriously going to make her marry that man, after everything that's happened?

IMRAN: Everything that's happened?

AMIRA: What he did to me.

IMRAN: What he did to you?

AMIRA: Yes.

IMRAN: He didn't do anything to you, you said so yourself.

AMIRA: How can you not see what's going on?

IMRAN: What's going on. Oh, I can see what's going on, alright. I can see that you're trying to get my feckless son off the hook by backing his ridiculous story.

AMIRA: What, so I'm lying?

IMRAN: Well, you…

AMIRA: You're calling me a liar?

IMRAN: Look…

AMIRA: *(Louder.)* Are you calling me a liar?

IMRAN: Maybe if you'd been a bit more upset about it…

AMIRA: Sorry?

IMRAN: I'm just saying. It's a bit odd you didn't say anything about it at the time. And now this business with Damee, and suddenly…

AMIRA: Wait, you're victim shaming me?

IMRAN: Erm…

AMIRA: Because I didn't make a scene? Because I didn't choose to make an unpleasant situation even worse by drawing attention to it, embarrassing me, embarrassing you, opening the door to the gossips and the scandalmongers… because I chose to deal with it quietly, in my own way, the way that millions of women have to, when they face this crap every day of their lives, because of that I somehow imagined it? Or even worse, made it up?

IMRAN: There's no need to get all hysterical about it.

AMIRA: Hysterical? Wow.

IMRAN: OK not hysterical. Hysterical is the wrong word.

AMIRA: No, no. Hysterical is exactly the right word. The word that means no matter how much men abuse their power over women, it's always the crazy woman's fault.

IMRAN: He's a holy man, Amira! You can't seriously expect me to believe he's been trying it on with another man's wife.

AMIRA: What if you could see it with your own eyes?

IMRAN: How are you going to do that? Draw me a picture? Or did you record it on your phone? You should to post it on YouTube. Get plenty of hits there, I'm sure!

AMIRA: *(Ignoring him.)* What if I find you somewhere to hide, and I get him back in here, and he thinks it's just me and him alone…

IMRAN: Yes, and?

AMIRA: And then he does it again. Then what?

IMRAN: Then…then…nothing. Because nothing would happen.

AMIRA: So you want me to do it.

IMRAN: *(Shrugs.)* Don't care. Do what you like.

AMIRA: You want me to offer myself to that two-faced creep to prove to you what he's really like. Is that what it's going to take?

IMRAN: Fine! Yes. Do it! That's fine with me! And when nothing happens, which is what will happen, or not happen, then you can apologise to me, and to him, and beg forgiveness for ever doubting him.

AMIRA: Fine.

IMRAN: In fact, all of you can.

DARINA/MARIAM/KHALIL: Fine.

IMRAN: And when you've proved that he really is a holy man, you'll accept this marriage to Mariam and welcome him to the family with open arms.

AMIRA: *(To DARINA.)* Send him in.

DARINA: Really?

AMIRA: Yep. It's time to let the dog see the rabbit.

DARINA goes out.

(To KHALIL and MARIAM.) You two better leave too. You don't want to see this.

MARIAM hurries out. KHALIL stays. He wants to watch. AMIRA stares at him, and he leaves reluctantly.

SCENE 4

AMIRA: *(To IMRAN.)* You ready?

IMRAN: Can't wait.

AMIRA: Good. Get in the Louis Rose.

IMRAN: What?

AMIRA: He mustn't be able to see you.

IMRAN: But, in the Louis Rose? Isn't that a bit...

AMIRA: Oh, for goodness' sake, just get under there and be quiet!

He gets under the table.

IMRAN: Next time you say I never do anything for you, just remember this.

AMIRA: Now, I want you to prepare yourself for what you're about to hear.

IMRAN (OOV): Don't worry about me, I'll be fine.

AMIRA: Whatever I'm about to say, remember I'm only saying it to prove he's a fake. You just let me know as soon as you're convinced, and I'll stop. I don't want to take this any further than I have to, okay?

IMRAN (OOV): Okay.

AMIRA: You'll step in when you realise what he's really like?

IMRAN (OOV): I already know what he's really like.

AMIRA: Just say yes!

IMRAN (OOV): Yes!

AMIRA: Shhh!

IMRAN: Yes.

AMIRA: He's coming!

AMIRA sits on the edge of the table, composes herself. TARTUFFE comes in with USMAN.

TARTUFFE: I was told you wanted to see me?

AMIRA: That's right. I need to speak to you. Alone.

She gestures at the door. TARTUFFE closes it behind him.

I wanted to apologise about what happened the other day. Between us. I didn't mean to put you off. It was all just such a shock! And when Damee jumped out… I was so worried he was going to hurt you. I was so confused I didn't know what I was saying. But it turned out OK

in the end, didn't it? My husband doesn't suspect a
thing. He's even been saying we should spend *more* time
together. That's why I can be alone with you now, and we
don't have to worry about getting caught…

A beat. TARTUFFE looks over his shoulder, then back at AMIRA.

TARTUFFE: Are you talking to me?

AMIRA: Of course!

TARTUFFE: It's just…this is a bit of a turn around, that's all.

AMIRA: No, it's not.

TARTUFFE: Because before, when I…

AMIRA: *(Prompting.)* When you…?

TARTUFFE: When we were together and I…

AMIRA: You…?

TARTUFFE: Exactly. I got the impression that you weren't…

AMIRA: Oh but I was.

TARTUFFE: Really?

AMIRA: Definitely. I mean, when you…

TARTUFFE: When I…

AMIRA: *(Encouraging.)* Yup…

TARTUFFE: When I…touched your breast…

AMIRA: *(Loudly.)* There it is!

She looks around for IMRAN to come out. Nothing.

TARTUFFE: When I touched your breast I got the impression
you didn't like it.

AMIRA: Well that's not... I mean, what woman wouldn't like it when a man like you touches her breast?

TARTUFFE considers this – he thinks she has a point. But then he remembers...

TARTUFFE: Hmmm. *(Beat.)* But you said I was a gropey little letch.

AMIRA: I meant in a good way!

TARTUFFE: There's a good way?

AMIRA is floundering.

AMIRA: Er...well...

TARTUFFE: I'm sorry, I think I should...

He turns to and heads for the door...

AMIRA: No, wait. You see, I was trying to hide how I really feel...

AMIRA has an idea.

For if that which the heart truly feels,
Perforce cannot for now be revealed,
Then, beneath our words, must it stay concealed.

TARTUFFE freezes in his tracks.

TARTUFFE: Oh!

He turns back.

So then...?

AMIRA: So then...
Though I may indeed have called you letch,
When you did *(loud)* wantonly grope my breast!

AMIRA is checking for IMRAN. Still no sign of him.

83

TARTUFFE: Yes?

AMIRA: Er… Do not believe that is how I really think of you,
    For, in fact, you must see that…

TARTUFFE: …the opposite is true?

AMIRA: Exactly!

TARTUFFE hurries over to her, excited.

TARTUFFE: So if you were to call me a fool you would mean…

AMIRA: I think you're cool?

TARTUFFE: And if you say, you think I'm lewd.

AMIRA: It means I think you're a dude.

TARTUFFE: Then tell me again what you think of me,
    Declaim what you hold Tartuffe to be,
    For now I know your true intent,
    Shall I only hear what is really meant!

AMIRA: You want me to…?

TARTUFFE nods eagerly. AMIRA shrugs.

OK.

(Loudly – for IMRAN.) Tartuffe is a creep!

TARTUFFE: I am sweet!

AMIRA: He's a sham!

TARTUFFE: I have charm!

AMIRA: He's a lying, scheming, filthy wretch!

TARTUFFE: *(Gasps.)* My God! You think Tartuffe's a catch!

AMIRA is checking for IMRAN – still not coming out.

AMIRA: He is a godless, filthy perve!

Unseen by AMIRA, TARTUFFE has come up right behind her. She turns and he's right there, in her face.

TARTUFFE: I am the godfather of lurve!

AMIRA slides away from him. He follows her.

Then are all my dearest hopes made real,
That you should feel the way I feel,
And knowing that you feel the same,
Does all the more my passions inflame,
I want to touch you, I want to feel you,
I want to smell you, I want to peel you…

He mimes undressing her.

AMIRA: Well let's not get too…

TARTUFFE: I want to taste you, I want to suck you,
    I want to thrill you, I want to f…

AMIRA: OK, that's pretty clear. I think we get the message.
    (Loudly – for IMRAN.) I don't think anyone could be in any
    doubt about what it is you want to do.

She checks for IMRAN again – surely he'll be coming out now. But no.

TARTUFFE: Wait a minute.

AMIRA: What is it?

TARTUFFE: How do I know this isn't a trick?

AMIRA: What do you mean?

TARTUFFE: How do I know you're not just saying this stuff to
    get me to agree to break off the marriage to whatsername?

AMIRA: Mariam.

TARUFFE: Exactly.

AMIRA: I'm not just saying it, trust me. I really mean it. Every word of it!

A beat.

TARTUFFE: Prove it.

AMIRA: Hmmm?

TARTUFFE: Enough talk. It's time for action.

AMIRA: What, now?

TARTUFFE: Yeah. Come on…

He starts unbuttoning his shirt.

AMIRA: Woah! OK, so we're going to do it right now are we? Here, on the Louis Rose? *(Louder for IMRAN's benefit.)* ON THE LOUIS ROSE?

TARTUFFE: We can talk about it all day, but the only way to prove you want me is to give yourself to me completely! I won't be convinced of your love until our bodies are blended together in…

He starts pulling down his trousers. AMIRA coughs to alert IMRAN.

…blended together in the ecstasy of…

His foot's stuck in his trouser leg and he hops around, off balance.

Bloody skinny jeans! Don't worry, they'll be off in a moment, and then we can start the blending!

AMIRA coughs louder.

AMIRA: You're so impulsive…maybe we should slow down a bit? Give ourselves a chance to relax and get in the mood.

TARTUFFE: I'm already in the mood. Let's do it.

AMIRA: Wait!

TARTUFFE: What?

AMIRA: If we give ourselves to each other, surely we'll be offending Allah? I know how close you and Him are...

TARTUFFE: Trust me, Allah won't get in our way.

AMIRA: But what about the whole sin of adultery thing?

TARTUFFE: OK, yes, generally speaking, Allah is against some types of...pleasure. But there are certain interpretations of the scripture that allow a bit of leeway where this kind of thing is concerned.

AMIRA: Are there?

TARTUFFE: Oh yes.

He finally manages to takes off his trousers.

Aha!

He waves the trousers above his head and throws them across the room. He starts to approach her, lasciviously.

You see, many scholars now believe that any sin can be counterbalanced as long as the motives of the sinners are pure and innocent.

AMIRA: And are your motives pure and innocent?

TARTUFFE: Definitely not...

He climbs onto the table with her. AMIRA coughs louder still.

That's a nasty cough you've got there.

AMIRA: Yes, it's very painful.

TARTUFFE: I've got a Fisherman's Friend in my jacket?

AMIRA: I might need a bit more than that.

She coughs again, tries knocking on the table.

TARTUFFE: It's annoying isn't it?

AMIRA: Really annoying!

She bangs harder on the table.

TARTUFFE: You mustn't feel guilty about this. The only problem we'd have is if someone found out. And no one's going to find out, are they? *(AMIRA looks down at the table, still no sign of IMRAN.)*

AMIRA: Apparently not. Well, then, I suppose there's no reason for me not to give in to this. I know it's wrong and it's not what I had in mind, but you need more proof, so… *(Louder, for IMRAN's benefit.)* If that's what you want!

TARTUFFE: *(Thinking she's talking to him.)* It certainly is! *(He lowers himself onto her.)*

AMIRA: Wait! Just check there's no one upstairs!

TARTUFFE: There isn't!

AMIRA: But what if my husband comes back FROM WHEREVER HE IS AT THE MOMENT?

TARTUFFE: Why are you worried about him? He thinks I'm like a like an actual angel. I can do no wrong. He could see us going at it like a pair of horny jack rabbits and still not believe it! Twat!

AMIRA: Just check one last time. For me!

TARTUFFE goes off to check. IMRAN crawls out from under the table.

Oh, nice of you to turn up.

IMRAN: That man is a disgrace!

AMIRA: You think?

IMRAN: I can't believe he'd do this to me. To you!

AMIRA: Is he going to do it though? Why don't you get back in there and wait 'til he's finished, just to make absolutely sure?

IMRAN: What an evil little bastard!

AMIRA: Are you not jumping to conclusions here? Give him a bit more time, he might redeem himself again.

As TARTUFFE comes back in, shutting the door behind him, AMIRA pushes IMRAN behind the curtains, gets back on the table.

TARTUFFE: *(Not seeing IMRAN.)* I've checked, there's no one out there. I'm aching for you, Amira, beautiful, amazing Amira, this is our moment, our chance, our time to finally, blissfully, rapturously… Oh just get your knickers off!

TARTUFFE climbs on the table. IMRAN steps out.

IMRAN: Put your pecker away, holy man!

TARTUFFE scrambles and falls off the table.

TARTUFFE: Ah!

AMIRA gets off the table and calmly adjusts her clothing.

It's not what it looks like!

AMIRA: It pretty much is.

TARTUFFE: *(To AMIRA.)* Wait, did you know he was…?

She nods and shrugs.

AMIRA: Sorry.

IMRAN: Marry my daughter and shag my wife? That's your game is it? I knew there was something wrong with you all along. I was just waiting for the proof, and now I've got it.

TARTUFFE: *(To IMRAN.)* Wait, you think I was…?

89

IMRAN: Please. Spare me any more of your bullshit.

TARTUFFE: But if you'd just let me explain…

IMRAN grabs him by the lapels and hauls him up so they are face to face.

IMRAN: I said enough! Get your stuff and get out of my house, right now, before I personally kick your not-so-holy backside all the way from here to Small Heath.

A beat.

TARTUFFE: I don't think so.

IMRAN: What?

TARTUFFE: I mean, it's not your house, is it?

IMRAN: *(Oops.)* What?

IMRAN puts TARTUFFE down and lets go of his lapels.

TARTUFFE: Correct me if I'm wrong, but this house belongs to me now.

AMIRA: *(To IMRAN.)* What?

TARTUFFE: So, if anyone is going to be leaving, it's going to be you. All of you.

IMRAN: Now hang on a minute…

TARTUFFE: Usman! You're about to find out what happens to people who cross me. Usman! Oh, yes I know how to deal with people like you, people who lie and cheat and try to trick honest servants of Allah! *(He picks up his trousers.)* You'll rue the day you questioned my piety!

He leaves.

SCENE 5

AMIRA: The house belongs to him? What's he talking about?

IMRAN: I don't want to tell you.

AMIRA: Tell me.

IMRAN: I think I might have done something really stupid.

AMIRA: Just tell me.

IMRAN: I'm so ashamed.

AMIRA: Imran, I'm your wife, and I love you. Whatever it is, I'm sure it can't be that bad.

IMRAN: I signed the house and the business over to him.

AMIRA: *(Shouts.)* You idiot!

IMRAN: *(Nodding.)* He did say he was going to use it to do the work of Allah. I thought…

AMIRA: Be quiet now…

IMRAN: Yup.

AMIRA: *(Thinking on her feet.)* We'll take him to court. We'll get it back, say you were incapacitated, mentally. They'll believe that.

IMRAN: We can't go to court.

AMIRA: Why not?

IMRAN: Because…the house and the business, that's not the worst bit.

AMIRA: That's *not* the worst bit?

IMRAN: He knows something about me. Something nobody else knows.

AMIRA: What?

IMRAN hurries to the door.

IMRAN: It's upstairs – we've got to stop him getting his hands on it!

He rushes out. AMIRA looks puzzled. IMRAN comes back in.

Come on!

AMIRA jumps up and follows him out.

ACT V

SCENE 1

Some time later. KHALIL and AMIRA in the living room. AMIRA sits with her head in her hand. IMRAN comes through, is about to go out the other door, then stops, considers something for a second, and hurries back the way he came. As he reaches the door he stops again, turns, mutters something under his breath and heads in the opposite direction again.

KHALIL: What are you doing?

IMRAN: I don't know.

KHALIL: Why don't we just take a time out and calmly discuss the best way to deal with this?

IMRAN: You don't understand. There was a box upstairs in my study…and now Tartuffe has it.

KHALIL: What was in it?

AMIRA: His father's fake passport.

KHALIL looks at IMRAN.

IMRAN: My father was an illegal immigrant.

KHALIL: I had no idea.

IMRAN: Yeah well it's not something you put on your 'Eid-al-Adha' roundrobin email, is it?

KHALIL: No, I suppose not. But your father, Allah bless his soul, passed away years ago. They can hardly deport him.

IMRAN: Not him, no.

He glances at AMIRA.

IMRAN: My British passport was issued on the basis of Dad's indefinite leave to remain. Without that my passport's invalid. So are the kids'. They can stick us all back on a flight to Pakistan tomorrow.

KHALIL: Would they do that?

IMRAN: Do you ever watch the news? 'Windrush' mean anything to you?

KHALIL: Yes I know, but if you contact the relevant authorities then they'll…

IMRAN: 'Hostile Environment'. Isn't that what they call it?

KHALIL: But surely, lessons have been learned…

IMRAN: Oh we've learned the lesson alright. It's 'keep Britain for the British, there ain't no black in the union jack'.

KHALIL: *(To himself.)* How did we get here?

IMRAN: I should never have voted 'Leave'.

KHALIL: This is bad. The fact that you kept the incriminating passport, and the fact that you then entrusted it to Tartuffe, both of these things, if you don't mind me saying, were mistakes on your part.

AMIRA: Do you think?

KHALIL: I do. Now he has complete control over you, you see? I get now why you were running around panicking a minute ago. It's a perfectly understandable reaction to a disaster of this magnitude.

IMRAN: Thanks. I feel a lot better knowing you understand.

AMIRA: There must be a way out of this.

IMRAN: There isn't. I've signed all the paperwork. I've *signed* it!

SCENE 2

MARIAM enters. IMRAN looks at MARIAM.

IMRAN: Hello beti.

MARIAM: Hi.

IMRAN: I'm so sorry. *(MARIAM nods. He moves towards her, hands stretched out. She moves away.)* I thought I was helping you. *(He turns to AMIRA.)* I thought I was helping all of us.

AMIRA nods.

AMIRA: Oh so…it's okay now.

IMRAN: What do you mean?

AMIRA: All the shitty things you've said to us. All the shouting and banging the table and the… *(Turning to MARIAM.)* What was it?

MARIAM: Patriarchal heteronormative posturing.

AMIRA: What she said.

IMRAN: Bilkul, you're right, I know, and I'm not asking you to forget it, but it's over now. *(To MARIAM.)* I promise. *(To KHALIL.)* I'm done with them. That's it. The holier-than-thou, pompous, piety-badge-wearing lot of them can all go to hell in a Nissan Micra.

KHALIL: Alright, steady on now… Nissan Micra…

IMRAN: No, Khalil, I'm serious. Religion is the problem here. And I'm having nothing more to do with it.

KHALIL: Imran…

IMRAN: No more fasting. No more zakat! And I'm not giving any more money to the mosque's new roof fund, either!

AMIRA: Why do you have to lurch from one extreme to the other? Just because you've been had by one fake holy man, doesn't mean they're all like that, does it?

KHALIL: Amira's absolutely right. We should take as our theme the concept of moderation in all…

AMIRA: Not now, Khalil.

KHALIL: …sure, no problem.

DAMEE enters, riled up, and DARINA.

DAMEE: Where is he?

KHALIL: Who?

DAMEE: Tartuffe! Darina said he's trying to get all our money with some kind of 'extortion racket'.

KHALIL: He's not extorting anything.

DAMEE: Oh right.

KHALIL: Extortion involves a threat of violence. What he's doing is blackmail.

DAMEE: I'll kill him!

DARINA and AMIRA restrain him.

AMIRA: Calm down, Damee.

DAMEE: Don't tell me to calm down…

AMIRA: We're civilized people…

DAMEE: I'm not!

AMIRA: We don't solve our problems by beating up anyone we don't like. This isn't Syria!

DARINA: Or Scotland.

AMIRA: And it's not Tartuffe you're angry with, is it?

DAMEE looks at her.

Don't worry. You're not the only one.

DAMEE notices IMRAN. They look at each other.

IMRAN: Hello son.

DAMEE: So, what, I'm part of the family again, am I?

IMRAN shrugs. He holds out his arms. DAMEE looks to AMIRA for a lead. She nods at him – it's okay to forgive IMRAN. DAMEE grabs IMRAN's hand and gives him a macho hug-cum-body bump, in the accepted way for sportsmen (and other men concerned about heteronormativity) to express affection.

IMRAN: *(Weakly.)* I've been very stressed lately.

DAMEE: Yeah, you and me both.

SCENE 3

DADIMAA comes in with the musicians – they're playing wedding music.

DADIMAA: Mubarak! Mubarak! *(Punjabi.)* It's time to celebrate the good news!

IMRAN: *(To musicians.)* Stop! Stop that!

The musicians stop.

(To DADIMAA.) What are you doing?

DADIMAA: What do mean what am I doing, I'm celebrating the wedding! My granddaughter is marrying Tahir Arsuf! Shaadi!

The musicians start playing again.

IMRAN: No, she's not. *(To musicians.)* Just be quiet a minute, stop. Stop!

They stop.

She's not marrying him. Tartuffe's a fake, he's trying to ruin us.

DADIMAA: What!

IMRAN: Yeah, I know! I took him in when he was practically begging on the streets... I treated him like a son, offered him everything I've got. Everything.

He looks at MIRIAM.

And he showed his gratitude by trying to f... *(remembers who he's talking to)* foist his attentions on my wife, and threatening to put me out on the street, broke. Like he was when I found him.

DARINA puts her arm round him.

DARINA: Is okay, you were huge Supak but we are here for you.

A beat.

DADIMAA: Well I don't believe any of it. Hit the beat!

The musicians start playing again.

IMRAN: If you don't shut the hell up right now I'll shove those bloody tablas right up your...

The musicians stop playing.

DADIMAA: Tariq Arsuf would never do such things. This is tall poppy syndrome – 'laalch buri balaa hai'. You're jealous of him because he's a better man than you are.

IMRAN: What? No I'm not. And no he isn't!

DADIMAA: Poor Tahir Arsuf! Stuck in this *(thrown at DARINA)* untidy house full of strange people *(thrown at AMIRA)* who all hate him. I know exactly how he feels…

IMRAN: Have you listened to a word I've said?

DADIMAA: …but false accusations won't worry him. 'Saanch ko aanch nahi' – 'pure gold does not fear the flame!'

IMRAN: Mum, I saw him with my own eyes…

DADIMAA: 'Naach na Jaane, aagan tedha' – 'a bad workman blames his tools.'

IMRAN: *(To DADIMAA.)* That doesn't even make sense! Look, I saw him trying it on with Amira, okay! I caught him, red-handed. With his trousers down. There, I've said it. I didn't want to spell it out for you, but if that's the only way you'll get it…

DADIMAA wags a finger at him.

DADIMAA: 'Ek myaan mein do talawaren nahi samaati.'

IMRAN: I saw him! Watch my lips: I-saw-him! Do you want me to draw you a picture?

DADIMAA: 'Iohe ke chane chabana.'

IMRAN: It's like trying to have a conversation with a Pakistani fridge magnet! The guy has assaulted my wife!

DADIMAA: Nahin! I won't hear any more of this.

She covers her ears.

IMRAN: If you weren't my mother…

DARINA: *(To IMRAN.)* Is frustrating. When someone will not believe you, even when you are explain whole thing to them over and over again. I can't imagine how that is feeling.

99

AMIRA: Dadimaa, we're in a lot of trouble. Imran has signed over the house and the business to Tartuffe. He's threatening to evict us.

DADIMAA: Nonsense.

IMRAN: It's true, dammit.

DADIMAA: I'm sure you're overreacting.

AMIRA: And he's got hold of your late husband's passport. He knows it's a fake.

IMRAN: He could have us deported back to Pakistan, for God's sake.

DADIMAA: Pakistan is not so bad. Might be good for you.

IMRAN: When I say us, I mean you too.

DADIMAA: Hai!! He is monster! We have to stop the wedding!

At the mention of the word 'wedding', the musicians start playing again.

DADIMAA: *(To musicians, in Punjabi.)* Shut up you idiot bunch of bastards!

The musicians stop playing.

SCENE 4

TARTUFFE enters with his assistant, USMAN, and a satchel with some paperwork.

TARTUFFE: What are you lot still doing here? I thought you'd have packed up and gone by now.

IMRAN: We're not going anywhere!

TARTUFFE: This eviction notice says you are.

He hands IMRAN a piece of paper.

DAMEE: That's it, I really am gonna kill him this time!
(Realising nobody's restraining him.) Don't try and stop me!

As if responding to a cue, KHALIL and AMIRA jump forward to restrain him. TARTUFFE addresses his bearded assistant, USMAN.

TARTUFFE: Usman, send out the following tweet: 'Tartuffe has moved. Housewarming party, all righteous people welcome to pop in for tea and holy chit chat hashtag Tartuffe hashtag come-deen-with-me.'

AMIRA: *(To TARTUFFE.)* What have we done to deserve this?

TARTUFFE: Exactly. What have you done to deserve any of this?

He looks round at the big house.

The big house. The fancy clothes. Nice cars, restaurants, dinner parties with your gora friends. Look at you all, so smug. So entitled. Life's not so easy when you haven't got a gold-plated pot to piss in, is it?

SCENE 5

WAQAAS comes in.

MARIAM: Waqaas!

WAQAAS: Mariam! What do mean the wedding's...
(Remembers his manners.) Oh, Salaam Aleikum.

ALL: Waleikum Asalaam.

WAQAAS: What do you mean the wedding's cancelled?

MARIAM: Did you get my texts?

WAQAAS: What texts?

His phone pings. He reads the text quickly.

WAQAAS: They know he's a fraud?

ALL: Yes, we know, etc.

TARTUFFE: Yes they know I'm a fraud.

Phone pings again.

WAQAAS: You're getting evicted?

ALL: Yes.

TARTUFFE: Yes, they're getting evicted.

Phone pings again.

WAQAAS: You're getting deported!

ALL: Yes.

TARTUFFE: Inshallah.

WAQAAS: Ooh. So that's why the police are outside.

ALL: Yes.

(A beat.) What/The police!/Oh my God! Etc.

IMRAN: That's it then. We're finished.

IMRAN collapses in a heap.

AMIRA: *(To TARTUFFE.)* So turning us out of our home and putting us on the street wasn't enough for you, is that it?

TARTUFFE holds up his hands.

TARTUFFE: Nothing to do with me.

DAMEE: You piece of shit!

DADIMAA: Hai!

DAMEE: Sorry Granny.

DADIMAA: Nahin. 'Shit' not strong enough. He's a two-faced Kanjri ka beta!

TARTUFFE: Well that's not very nice.

DAMEE lunges at him and is restrained by KHALIL.

IMRAN: Damee. Leave him. He's right. It's not his fault.

DAMEE: What?

IMRAN: If there's anyone to blame it's me. I've done this. It's my fault. No one else.

AMIRA: Come on, that's not true.

IMRAN: I've brought all this upon us by being a stupid, vain, pompous fool.

DARINA: OK some of that is true.

AMIRA: Darina!

DARINA: Just saying…

WAQAAS, waiting patiently, tries to get everyone back on message.

WAQAAS: *(Patiently.)* Sorry to interrupt. The police…?
(DARINA goes out to head them off.)

AMIRA: What are we going to do?

WAQAAS: It's not too late. I've got a car outside.

AMIRA: We can't run away.

DADIMAA: Don't listen to her! Let's go. Which one is it?

WAQAAS: It's the Kia Picanto.

DADIMAA: You couldn't get Mercedes?

MARIAM: *(Takes WAQAAS' hand.)* Let's go somewhere far away. Where we can disappear. Somewhere where they'll never find us!

WAQAAS: Yes! How about Bradford?

SCENE 6

DARINA shows three people in – an Asian PC, a white PC, and a white woman in plain clothes.

DARINA: Policemans is here.

PC KUMAR: Evening all!

PC PARRY: Evening all!

DARINA: Old-fashioned policemans.

PC KUMAR: PC Raj Kumar,

PC PARRY: PC Tom Parry,

BOTH: West Midlands Police.

DARINA leaves.

SARAH: I'm Sarah Wells from…

DAMEE decides to take charge.

DAMEE: Yeah very good. Listen boys, we're all Asian, innit.

PC PARRY: I'm not.

DAMEE: Yeah well ok but surely we can come to some kind of…

SARAH: Sorry, sir, I'm Sarah Wells…

DAMEE: Alright love, the mans are talking…

SARAH: I'm Detective Chief Inspector Sarah Wells,

SARAH/PC PARRY/PC KUMAR: West Midlands Police.

SARAH: I've come to talk to Mr. Imran Parvaiz.

DAMEE: *(Meekly.)* That's him.

DAMEE points at IMRAN. IMRAN looks shell-shocked. AMIRA takes his hand, supportively.

AMIRA: We can get through this.

IMRAN nods. He's suddenly calm.

IMRAN: You're right. *(To SARAH.)* I'm sorry Inspector. We'll be with you in a moment. *(To AMIRA.)* Listen, I'll deal with the police. I want you to go with Waqaas. Take my mother and the kids. Do you understand?

AMIRA: OK.

IMRAN: It's all going to be fine…

AMIRA: I know. I'll look after everyone. I don't want you to worry.

DAMEE and MARIAM come over and stand with AMIRA. She puts her arms round them.

AMIRA: We're going to be fine, aren't we?

They nod.

TARTUFFE: Ah, look Usman, look at the happy family.

SARAH is staring at USMAN.

SARAH: Detective Sergeant Ghul?

She looks to her colleagues, USMAN looks shifty.

It is him, isn't it?

PC KUMAR: Oh yeah! Look who it is.

PC PARRY: Oh yeah! Who is it?

PC KUMAR: Sergeant Ghul.

PC PARRY: Who?

PC KUMAR: From the thing.

PC PARRY: Oh yeah Ghully from the *thing*!

PC KUMAR: Innit. Ghully! Ghully! Ghully!

PC PARRY: Oi! Oi!…

He trails off as he catches SARAH glaring at him.

TARTUFFE: Usman?

USMAN realises his cover is blown. A beat.

USMAN: Hello Chief Inspector.

SARAH: We met at Bob Pinker's retirement do.

USMAN: That's right. *(Beat.)* How's it going?

SARAH: Good, thanks. You?

USMAN: Not bad. Just, you know, doing a bit of undercover work.

SARAH: Right.

PC KUMAR: Right.

PC PARRY: Classic Ghully.

TARTUFFE: Usman! What the hell are you talking about?

USMAN: I'm sorry Mr. Arsuf. I'm not who you think I am. I'm actually a police officer with the CTU. The Counter Terrorism Act of 2015 contains a duty on the authorities to have due regard to prevent people from being drawn into terrorism.

DAMEE: Shut up! He's fucking Prevent, innit!

DARINA: *(To audience.)* I was not expecting that, was you?

TARTUFFE: Wait, hang on a minute. I haven't done anything wrong.

IMRAN: Ha!

DAMEE: You done plenty, cuz.

TARTUFFE: Yes but not like that. *(To USMAN.)* I've just been helping these people find the comfort of Allah's love.

USMAN: You've been raising funds fraudulently.

TARTUFFE: It's going to charity!

IMRAN: Ha!

TARTUFFE: Yeah, OK, whatever. But it's not for bloody ISIS. *(To USMAN.)* Why do you care what I do with the money I raise? I'm doing the work of Allah. You don't ask the Archbishop of Canterbury what he does with his collection tin.

USMAN goes to grab TARTUFFE. He takes a defensive stance.

Back off, guy!

USMAN looks at PC KUMAR.

USMAN: Give us a hand?

PC KUMAR steps forward and grabs TARTUFFE.

TARTUFFE: *(All trace of Arabic accent gone.)* Get your hands off me, bro! I'm not radicalizing nobody, man. I'm not even religious. I'm faking it. *(To IMRAN.)* Tell him I'm faking it!

IMRAN says nothing.

(To AMIRA.) Tell him!

AMIRA looks away. TARTUFFE looks at the family.

You people make me sick! Making out you're such
upstanding decent members of the community…then the
first chance you get to shaft me… *(Makes shafting gesture.)*
You know what you are? You're hypocrites!

He turns to the police officers.

Look, I've done some things, maybe stretched the truth
here and there maybe let people think I'm a holy man,
but I'm just trying to make a living.

A beat.

Look at me. A poor uneducated Paki from Small Heath.
Nobody. Who does someone like me get to be in this
country? Prime Minister? Head of the Bank of England?
Director General of the BBC? Those people don't look
like me. None of them. So what am I left with. Taxi
driver? Shelf stacker? Maybe a jacked up Jihadi going out
to Syria to wave a gun around like it's *Call of Duty.* Or
maybe this guy *(indicates himself)* with the beard, and the
clothes. Now I look like 'a Muslim'. The more different I
am the better you like it. And suddenly I'm not invisible.
Suddenly people want to know about me. Put out some
pamphlets. Some shit on Twitter. Next thing you know,
you've got 'followers'. You're in the local papers. On the
radio. I've even been on *Newsnight.*

WAQAAS: *(Impressed.)* I love *Newsnight.*

TARTUFFE: I think you can still catch it on iPlayer.

PC KUMAR takes hold of his arm.

Were you not listening? You've got the wrong guy.

USMAN: They all say that.

He goes out with PC KUMAR and USMAN.

TARTUFFE: *(To family.)* I'll be fine, thanks for asking. I'll send you a postcard from Guantanamo Bay! *(To SARAH.)* I'm not an extremist, I'm a con man. Jacob Rees Mogg's an extremist, why aren't you arresting that fucked-up bitch!

As he goes out of the room he pockets a small silver cigar box.

(To USMAN.) You know I'll be out in a week, man. I'll get the *Guardian* to livestream my Twitter feed... *(To IMRAN.)* You should be thanking me for what I've done for your fucked-up family, you fat bastard! *(To AMIRA.)* And I know you wanted it. *(To MARIAM.)* And good luck marrying *that* pussy!

SCENE 7

He exits with the police. A beat. IMRAN turns to SARAH.

IMRAN: Thank you, Detective Inspector. I'm sorry you had to hear that.

SARAH: Oh that's not why I'm here.

IMRAN: Oh.

SARAH: I came to speak to you.

IMRAN: Oh. I see.

AMIRA takes his hand.

But let me make something perfectly clear. If there is an illegal immigrant here, and I'm not saying there is, but if there is, then it's me.

SARAH: It's you?

IMRAN: Yeah, it's me. No one else. Not my family. They know nothing about any of it.

SARAH: That you're an illegal immigrant?

IMRAN: That's right. Got it?

SARAH: OK. I don't know anything about that... I came to book a venue for the Annual Police Ball? They said I should come and talk to you.

IMRAN and AMIRA exchange a relieved look.

IMRAN: *(To SARAH.)* Oh. I see! Well I'm sure we can help you with that!

SARAH: Great!

IMRAN: Just email me with the details...

He hands her his business card.

SARAH: Great! *(Beat.)* Er, they also said something about a discount...?

IMRAN: No problem, no problem. Special rates for the boys in blue.

SARAH: And girls!

IMRAN: And girls!

They all laugh. Release of tension. She heads out, stops.

SARAH: Sorry, what was all that stuff about an illegal immigrant?

ALL: Nothing!

SARAH: Right!

SARAH leaves. Awkward moment.

IMRAN: Vah! That was easy! Not easy. Obviously he's... I mean, I could have said something, but...you've got to play the game right? We're little pieces. And we're okay now. Not ok, but...we're all sorted. Are we all sorted?

AMIRA: No.

IMRAN: No, we're not. Why not?

AMIRA: We'll need to check the dates with Mariam first.

IMRAN: Do we?

AMIRA: She needs to choose the date for her wedding reception. Her and Waqaas.

IMRAN: Oh. Yes. Of course.

MARIAM and WAQAAS look at each other, and then hug.

(To AMIRA.) I was going to say that.

WAQAAS: Thank you, Mr. Pervaiz! Trust me, your daughter will be happy with me. Our journey together will be long and full of intellectual vigour, and you won't ever regret setting us off on this amazing voyage of discovery!

He hugs IMRAN.

IMRAN: I'm regretting it already.

DADIMAA: *(To MARIAM.)* I hope you don't think you can arrange a wedding on your own? I need to see the guest list to check it...

MARIAM: Of course, Dadimaa, your word will be final...

The rest of the cast and chorus sing Punjabi wedding song 'Chitta kukkar' through the following.

MARIAM: Lights down low, it's the end credits.

DAMEE: I come full blown to make amends, spread it...

MARIAM: Policeman come an apprehend the beast...

DAMEE: Trend on Twitter, like a false belief
But he talked bare shit...

111

MARIAM: Better brush his teeth,
    Swear Pakistan Man's from Small Heath…

DAMEE/MARIAM: Best believe…

DAMEE: Man like me come flowing
    There's an 'S' on my chest that's showing
    And it's glowing

MARIAM: Woman like me come flowing
    There's an 'S' on my chest that's showing
    And it's glowing

MARIAM/DAMEE: Woman/Man like me come flowing
    There's an 'S' on my chest that's showing
    And it's glowing

MARIAM: Cos I came home
    Like the Lone Ranger
    I called out this clone faker
    Saw through his lies like his dad
    Was a glassmaker
    Schooled the fed
    They should call me a caretaker

DAMEE: The kid is back
    I'm a heartbreaker
    Without me, you see
    There's no harmony
    A young couple in love
    Where's the bride-to-be
    They done got cockblocked
    By Tartuffegee
    Now's he's in the copshop
    With West Mids Police
    And me, you see
    I'm just chillin'
    Now the wedding's coming

Top billing
I'm killing
A million hearts
Yes I'm breaking
Cos now Zainab's mine
For the taking…

*He leaves with the rest of the family and chorus. DARINA enters
with a cleaning bucket and Marigolds.*

DARINA: *(To audience.)* So, is all OK. Family is stay together,
and bad person is sent into wilderness. Well, Small Heath.
And what is moral of the story? Don't listen to false
prophet? Don't let other peoples get between you and
your God? Don't follow leaders, watch parking meters?
Maybe. But think about this: we live in strange times…
everybody wants to be themself, but nobody knows who
they are anymore. Are you man? Woman? Black? White?
Muslim, Christian, Jew, Citizen of World, Europe, British,
English, Brummie? Is changing all the time. So for me,
moral of story is this: be good to your *cleaner*, because she
knows where your passport is!

END.

Richard Pinto is a British writer. For radio he co-created and wrote *ElvenQuest* with Anil Gupta, and he was the lead writer on both the radio and the TV series of *Goodness Gracious Me*. Other television writing credits include *Small Potatoes*, *The Kumars at No. 42*, *Bromwell High*, *Mutual Friends*, *Fresh Meat*, *Armstrong and Miller*, *Citizen Khan* and *Boomers*.

Anil Gupta is a British comedy writer and producer. He has produced many shows on radio and television including *Goodness Gracious Me*, the spoof chat show *The Kumars at No. 42*, *The Office*, *Citizen Khan* and *Bromwell High*. He wrote the Cinderella episode of the 2008 comedy drama series *Fairy Tales*, and *ElvenQuest*.